I0007644

Configuration Management Protocols: TFTP, SCP, and Beyond

James Relington

Copyright © 2025 James Relington

All rights reserved

DEDICATION

To those who seek knowledge, inspiration, and new perspectives—
may this book be a companion on your journey, a spark for curiosity,
and a reminder that every page turned is a step toward discovery.

AKNOWLEDGEMENTS

I would like to express my deepest gratitude to everyone who contributed to the creation of this book. To my colleagues and mentors, your insights and expertise have been invaluable. A special thank you to my family and friends for their unwavering support and encouragement throughout this journey.

Introduction to Configuration Management Protocols

Configuration management is an essential aspect of network administration that ensures the proper operation and security of network devices and systems. By controlling the configuration of hardware, software, and network elements, organizations can ensure that systems remain operational, secure, and efficient. The primary purpose of configuration management protocols is to facilitate the transfer, management, and backup of configuration files, enabling network administrators to maintain consistent configurations across devices. These protocols play a critical role in streamlining processes and improving the overall reliability of network infrastructures.

One of the most significant challenges in network management is ensuring that configuration files across a network of devices remain synchronized. A network may consist of hundreds or even thousands of devices, such as routers, switches, firewalls, and servers, each requiring consistent and up-to-date configuration files. Without a proper management system in place, network administrators may face difficulties in maintaining device configurations, leading to performance issues, security vulnerabilities, and the inability to recover from failures. Configuration management protocols help solve these problems by providing standardized ways of transferring and managing configuration files, ensuring uniformity and reducing human error.

At the core of configuration management are protocols that enable the reliable transfer of configuration files between devices and central management systems. Among the most commonly used protocols in this domain are Trivial File Transfer Protocol (TFTP), Secure Copy Protocol (SCP), and Secure File Transfer Protocol (SFTP). Each of these protocols offers unique benefits and addresses different needs in the network management process. While TFTP is a lightweight protocol often used for transferring configuration files and firmware in environments where security is not a primary concern, SCP and SFTP provide encrypted, secure file transfers for environments that require higher levels of security. Understanding the functionalities and differences between these protocols is essential for network administrators to select the appropriate protocol based on their specific needs.

The Trivial File Transfer Protocol (TFTP) is one of the oldest and most widely used protocols for transferring files across a network. It is known for its simplicity and ease of implementation, which makes it a popular choice in environments where security is less of a concern. TFTP operates over the User Datagram Protocol (UDP), which means it does not establish a connection before transferring data. This lightweight nature allows TFTP to be fast and efficient, but it also means that TFTP lacks many features found in more robust file transfer protocols, such as error recovery and encryption. Despite its limitations, TFTP remains widely used in environments like embedded systems, routers, and network devices, where the simplicity and speed of file transfers are prioritized.

In contrast to TFTP, Secure Copy Protocol (SCP) offers a more secure approach to file transfers. SCP operates over the Secure Shell (SSH) protocol, which provides encryption to protect the integrity and confidentiality of the transferred data. SCP is commonly used for transferring configuration files in environments where security is critical, such as enterprise networks and data centers. The key advantage of SCP over TFTP is its ability to securely authenticate users, encrypt files during transmission, and ensure that files are not tampered with during transfer. However, SCP's reliance on SSH means that it may be slightly more complex to configure and requires a secure SSH setup on both the source and destination devices.

Secure File Transfer Protocol (SFTP) is another widely used protocol that offers encryption and authentication features similar to SCP but with additional capabilities. SFTP provides a more robust and flexible method for securely transferring files over a network. Unlike SCP, which is designed specifically for file transfers, SFTP is a comprehensive file transfer protocol that allows for a range of file operations, including file manipulation and directory listing. SFTP is built on the SSH protocol, ensuring secure file transfers, and it supports features such as file access control, resuming interrupted transfers, and performing operations on remote files. These features make SFTP an ideal choice for managing configurations in environments where file integrity and security are top priorities.

The use of these protocols in configuration management is not limited to just transferring configuration files. They also enable network administrators to automate many aspects of configuration management, such as backing up device configurations and synchronizing configurations across a network of devices. Automation tools can leverage these protocols to schedule regular backups, compare configurations, and even push updates to devices automatically, significantly reducing the workload for administrators and minimizing the risk of human error. For example, administrators can use SCP or SFTP to automatically back up the configuration of a router every night, ensuring that the most up-to-date configuration is always available in case of a device failure or configuration corruption.

One of the key benefits of configuration management protocols is the ability to maintain consistent and standardized configurations across all devices in a network. This standardization ensures that devices are configured according to the organization's policies, security requirements, and operational guidelines. It also allows administrators to quickly and easily roll back to a previous configuration in the event of a problem, making it much easier to recover from misconfigurations or security breaches. Furthermore, configuration management protocols help organizations comply with various regulatory and industry standards, such as ISO 27001, HIPAA, and PCI-DSS, which require strict controls over system configurations.

However, as with any technology, there are challenges associated with the use of configuration management protocols. One of the most significant challenges is the complexity of managing configurations across large-scale networks. In large enterprises, where there may be hundreds or even thousands of devices to manage, it can be difficult to ensure that configurations are consistently applied and maintained across all devices. In such environments, network administrators may need to use advanced tools and strategies, such as configuration management platforms, version control systems, and automation scripts, to ensure that configurations are managed efficiently and accurately.

Another challenge is the potential security risks associated with configuration management protocols. While SCP and SFTP provide secure file transfers, TFTP is inherently insecure due to its lack of encryption and authentication. As a result, TFTP should only be used in trusted, closed environments where security is not a primary concern. In open or untrusted networks, it is essential to use secure protocols such as SCP or SFTP to ensure that configuration files are not intercepted, tampered with, or compromised during transmission.

Despite these challenges, the role of configuration management protocols in modern network management cannot be overstated. As networks continue to grow in complexity, the need for efficient, secure, and automated configuration management becomes more critical. By understanding the strengths and limitations of TFTP, SCP, and SFTP, network administrators can make informed decisions about which protocols to use for their specific needs. Ultimately, configuration management protocols are vital tools for ensuring the consistency, reliability, and security of network configurations, and they play a crucial role in maintaining the overall health of an organization's network infrastructure.

The Role of Configuration Management in Network Administration

Configuration management plays a pivotal role in the successful administration of network infrastructures. It involves the process of handling, controlling, and maintaining the configuration of network devices and systems, ensuring they remain consistent, secure, and functional. As networks grow in complexity, the need for structured and automated management of configurations becomes increasingly critical. Network administrators rely on configuration management to prevent errors, reduce downtime, and ensure compliance with organizational policies and industry regulations. Without proper configuration management, organizations can experience a host of issues ranging from performance degradation to severe security vulnerabilities.

The core purpose of configuration management is to maintain and enforce standardized device configurations across a network. A network may comprise routers, switches, firewalls, servers, and other devices, each of which needs to be configured with specific settings to perform its intended function. The configurations could include network settings, security policies, access control lists, routing protocols, and other operational parameters. Consistently managing these configurations is essential for the network to operate efficiently and securely. If these configurations are inconsistent, network performance can be impacted, leading to issues such as slow response times, network outages, or even data breaches.

One of the primary challenges in network administration is ensuring that configuration files across multiple devices are synchronized and up-to-date. In large-scale networks, maintaining configuration consistency can become a daunting task. Without a formal configuration management process, administrators may struggle to ensure that the devices across the network are running the same version of software and configuration settings. This can result in discrepancies, where some devices may be running outdated or incompatible configurations. Such inconsistencies can cause connectivity issues, security risks, and operational inefficiencies. Configuration management provides a framework for standardizing configurations across all network devices, reducing the likelihood of errors and ensuring a smooth and seamless network operation.

Beyond maintaining consistency, configuration management also plays a critical role in network security. Secure configuration settings are vital for safeguarding a network from external and internal threats. Network devices often contain sensitive data and control mechanisms that need to be carefully configured to prevent unauthorized access and misuse. Without proper configuration management, network devices may be left with default passwords, insecure protocols, or unnecessary services that could be exploited by malicious actors. Configuration management ensures that devices are configured in accordance with security best practices, such as disabling unused ports, enforcing strong passwords, and ensuring that only necessary services are enabled. Additionally, it helps ensure that configuration changes are tracked and logged, providing an audit trail in case of security incidents or compliance checks.

Another important aspect of configuration management is its role in disaster recovery and business continuity. Configuration files are often the foundation of network device operation, and losing these files can result in significant downtime or even complete network failure. By maintaining regular backups of configuration files, administrators can quickly restore devices to their previous operational state in the event of a failure. Configuration management systems typically incorporate automated backup processes, ensuring that configuration files are securely stored and easily recoverable. In the event of hardware failure, misconfiguration, or software corruption, the ability to restore configurations from a backup can significantly reduce the time it takes to recover and get the network back online.

In addition to security and recovery, configuration management also contributes to operational efficiency. Managing a network requires constant updates, patches, and adjustments to configuration settings to accommodate new devices, applications, and services. Rather than manually configuring each device, configuration management allows administrators to automate and streamline these processes. Using configuration management tools, administrators can apply changes across multiple devices simultaneously, ensuring that the entire network is updated consistently and in a timely manner. This automation reduces the administrative burden, accelerates deployment times, and minimizes the risk of human error. Furthermore, the ability to automate routine configuration tasks allows administrators to focus on more strategic initiatives, improving overall productivity.

In large, dynamic networks, changes to configurations occur regularly, whether due to software updates, security patches, or new network devices being added. Configuration management helps to ensure that changes are tracked and controlled. Change management is a key component of configuration management, as it establishes procedures for implementing, reviewing, and approving changes to device configurations. By maintaining a detailed record of all configuration changes, administrators can trace any issues that arise to specific modifications, making it easier to troubleshoot problems. Additionally, change management helps prevent unauthorized changes, which could introduce security vulnerabilities or disrupt network operations. For organizations that need to comply with industry regulations or standards, such as ISO 27001 or HIPAA, having a robust configuration management system in place is essential for demonstrating compliance.

The integration of configuration management with network monitoring tools further enhances its effectiveness. While configuration management focuses on maintaining consistent configurations, monitoring tools provide real-time visibility into the health and performance of the network. By integrating these two functions, administrators can quickly identify any discrepancies between the actual network state and the desired configuration. For example, if a network device is found to be operating with an incorrect configuration, the monitoring system can alert the administrator, prompting them to take corrective action. This integration allows for proactive network management, where issues can be detected and addressed before they cause significant problems.

As network infrastructures continue to evolve, configuration management tools are becoming increasingly sophisticated. Many modern configuration management systems now offer features such as version control, which allows administrators to track and compare different versions of configuration files. This is particularly useful when rolling back to a previous configuration or auditing changes over time. In addition, some configuration management systems support cloud-based networks, enabling administrators to manage configurations across distributed environments and hybrid infrastructures. These advanced tools are making configuration management more scalable, flexible, and accessible, allowing network administrators to manage complex and diverse environments with ease.

The role of configuration management in network administration is not just about maintaining the functionality and security of individual devices. It is also about ensuring that the network as a whole operates efficiently, securely, and in alignment with the organization's strategic objectives. By implementing effective configuration management practices, organizations can enhance their network's reliability, reduce operational risks, and streamline administrative processes. In a world where network infrastructures are becoming increasingly complex, the importance of robust configuration management systems cannot be overstated. Through careful planning, automation, and monitoring, network administrators can harness the power of configuration management to support the ongoing success and growth of their organizations.

Overview of TFTP: Trivial File Transfer Protocol

The Trivial File Transfer Protocol, commonly referred to as TFTP, is one of the simplest and oldest file transfer protocols in use today. It was designed as a lightweight, easy-to-implement protocol for transferring files over a network, primarily used in environments where more sophisticated protocols like FTP are unnecessary or impractical. TFTP operates over the User Datagram Protocol (UDP), which provides a connectionless, minimal overhead transport layer. While it lacks many of the advanced features and security measures of other file transfer protocols, TFTP continues to be employed in specific scenarios where simplicity and speed are prioritized over security.

TFTP was originally developed in the 1980s as a simple alternative to the more complex File Transfer Protocol (FTP). Unlike FTP, which operates over a connection-oriented TCP (Transmission Control Protocol) layer, TFTP is designed to be as simple as possible. It does not require user authentication or advanced configuration, making it an ideal solution for devices that need to transfer small files quickly and without much overhead. Its simplicity, however, comes at the cost of features like encryption, error recovery, and file management capabilities, which are inherent to more advanced protocols like FTP or Secure Copy Protocol (SCP).

TFTP operates in a client-server model, where a client requests the transfer of a file from a server, or vice versa, over a network. The client sends a request for the file it needs, and the server responds by transferring the requested file. TFTP does not provide any built-in mechanism for establishing a secure connection or verifying the identity of the devices involved, making it susceptible to certain types of attacks, such as man-in-the-middle attacks. This lack of security is one of the key reasons why TFTP is typically only used in trusted, isolated networks or in environments where security concerns are minimal.

One of the key features of TFTP is its use of UDP as the transport protocol. UDP is a connectionless protocol, meaning that there is no need to establish a dedicated communication channel between the client and server before data transfer begins. This makes TFTP faster than protocols that rely on TCP, as there is less overhead associated with the initial connection setup. However, because UDP does not include any error correction mechanisms, TFTP must rely on its own application-level protocols to detect and handle errors. This is a limitation when compared to more robust protocols like FTP, which automatically handles errors and ensures reliable delivery of files.

TFTP is designed to be simple to implement and lightweight, making it a popular choice for embedded systems, network devices, and other environments where minimal configuration and low resource consumption are important. For example, network devices such as routers, switches, and firewalls often use TFTP to load firmware updates or configuration files from a centralized server. In these scenarios, the simplicity and speed of TFTP make it an attractive choice. Since these devices typically do not require user interaction or advanced file management, the lack of security features in TFTP is often not a significant concern.

Despite its advantages, TFTP has several notable limitations. The most significant drawback is its lack of security features. Because TFTP does not provide any form of encryption or authentication, the data being transferred can be intercepted or modified by unauthorized parties. This makes TFTP unsuitable for transferring sensitive information over open or untrusted networks. Furthermore, TFTP does not include any form of file integrity checking, so there is no built-in way to ensure that a file has been transferred correctly or has not been corrupted during the transfer. If a transfer is interrupted or an error occurs, the client will not receive any feedback from the server, making error recovery a manual process.

TFTP's lack of error checking and recovery mechanisms means that it is most appropriate for transferring small files in environments where the possibility of errors is minimal, or where the consequences of errors are not significant. It is commonly used in situations where a device needs to load a configuration file or firmware update from a server without the need for complex interaction. For instance, network administrators might use TFTP to remotely configure routers or switches by transferring configuration files from a central server to the device. The simplicity of TFTP allows administrators to quickly and efficiently update multiple devices in a network without the overhead of more complex protocols.

Another limitation of TFTP is its inability to transfer files larger than 32MB due to its use of a 16-bit block size. This limitation makes TFTP unsuitable for transferring larger files, such as software updates or large data sets, that exceed this size. In these cases, more advanced protocols such as FTP, SCP, or SFTP are typically used, as they are designed to handle larger files and provide more robust error handling and security features.

TFTP is also limited in its functionality compared to more feature-rich file transfer protocols. For example, TFTP does not provide support for directory listings or file manipulation. This means that TFTP cannot be used for tasks such as navigating file systems, renaming files, or deleting files. It is strictly designed for the transfer of files from one device to another, without any advanced file management capabilities. This simplicity is both an advantage and a limitation, depending on the requirements of the task at hand.

While TFTP may not be suitable for all file transfer needs, it remains a valuable tool in specific use cases. Its primary advantage is its speed and efficiency in transferring small files in trusted, controlled environments. For example, network devices that require regular firmware or configuration updates can use TFTP to quickly and efficiently download the necessary files. Additionally, TFTP is often used in bootstrapping scenarios, where devices need to retrieve an initial configuration or operating system image from a server when they are first powered on or reset.

TFTP's lack of security and error recovery features mean that it is best suited for environments where these factors are not a significant concern. In more secure environments, where sensitive data needs to be transferred or the risk of errors is higher, administrators will typically opt for more secure and robust protocols, such as SCP or SFTP. These protocols provide encryption, authentication, and error checking, making them better suited for transferring files over untrusted or open networks.

Despite its limitations, TFTP's simplicity and efficiency ensure that it remains a widely used protocol in certain network management and embedded system applications. For those who need a lightweight, no-frills solution for transferring configuration files or firmware updates in controlled environments, TFTP provides an ideal solution. While it may not be the most secure or feature-rich protocol, its role in specific use cases continues to be important in the broader landscape of file transfer protocols.

FTP Operational Mechanics: How It Works

The File Transfer Protocol, or FTP, is one of the oldest and most widely used protocols for transferring files between computers over a network. FTP operates over the Internet Protocol Suite and is commonly used to transfer large files, back up data, and exchange documents between clients and servers. Despite its age, FTP remains a fundamental component of modern network communication, providing an efficient and reliable method for transferring files across different types of networks. Understanding how FTP works involves examining its operational mechanics, including its underlying architecture, communication model, and how data is transferred between the client and the server.

FTP is built on a client-server model, where one machine acts as a client, and the other serves as the server. The client initiates requests to the server to either download files from or upload files to the server. To understand FTP's operation, it is important to recognize the two main channels that are established between the client and the server: the control channel and the data channel. The control channel is responsible for sending commands and receiving responses, while the data channel is used for the actual transfer of files. These two channels operate independently, with the control channel typically using port 21 and the data channel using a dynamic port for transferring the data itself.

When a client wants to initiate an FTP session, it connects to the server's control channel. The control channel is used to send commands, such as login credentials and file manipulation requests, and to receive responses from the server. Upon connecting, the client sends the server a command, often starting with the user's authentication details, such as the username and password. These authentication credentials are required to establish a valid session, though FTP does not encrypt them, making FTP vulnerable to certain types of attacks, such as packet sniffing. After successful authentication, the client can issue additional commands to the server, such as listing directories or requesting specific files for download.

Once the control connection is established and authentication is successful, the client can request to transfer files. To facilitate this transfer, FTP uses a second channel, the data channel, to carry the actual file content. The key difference between the control and data channels is that while the control channel remains open throughout the session, the data channel is established dynamically for each file transfer. When the client requests a file transfer, the server allocates a port for the data channel and communicates this port number back to the client over the control channel. The client then establishes a connection to the server's data port, and the file transfer begins.

FTP offers two modes for data transfer: active mode and passive mode. The primary difference between these two modes lies in the direction of the data channel connection and which machine is responsible for initiating it. In active mode, the client establishes a connection to the server's control port and issues commands. When the client requests a file transfer, the server opens a random port on its side and sends the data back to the client through this port. In this case, the server actively connects to the client's data port to begin the transfer. However, the issue with active mode is that it may be blocked by firewalls or network address translation (NAT) devices, which often prevent inbound connections to the client's machine.

To address this issue, passive mode was introduced. In passive mode, the situation is reversed: the client opens a data connection to the server rather than waiting for the server to initiate the connection. This mode is particularly useful in environments where the client is behind a firewall or NAT device, as the firewall would block the server's attempt to connect to the client. In passive mode, the server still opens a random port for data transfer, but instead of the server connecting to the client, the client initiates the connection to the server's chosen port. This ensures that the data channel is established without any interference from network devices, making passive mode the preferred choice in many modern networks.

FTP supports two primary file transfer modes: binary and ASCII. In binary mode, files are transferred as raw data, with each byte of the file being transmitted exactly as it is. This mode is typically used for transferring non-text files, such as images, videos, or software applications, where preserving the exact file content is critical. On the other hand, ASCII mode is used for transferring text files. In ASCII mode, the data is converted between the different character encoding formats used by different operating systems. This allows text files to be transferred correctly between machines running different operating systems, such as Windows and Unix, which may have different line endings. However, ASCII mode is not suitable for binary files, as the data may be corrupted due to character encoding conversions.

FTP does not provide encryption for the control or data channels, meaning that all communications, including usernames, passwords, and transferred data, are sent in clear text. This lack of encryption makes FTP insecure in environments where confidentiality is important. For this reason, many organizations and users prefer to use FTPS or SFTP, which are secure versions of FTP that add encryption to both the control and data channels. FTPS, or FTP Secure, extends FTP by adding the Secure Sockets Layer (SSL) or Transport Layer Security (TLS) protocols to provide encryption for the control channel, and in some cases, the data channel as well. SFTP, on the other hand, is an entirely different protocol based on SSH (Secure Shell) and provides a secure, encrypted connection for transferring files.

Despite its lack of security, FTP remains widely used due to its speed and efficiency in transferring large files. Its relatively simple design allows it to operate across different network environments and be easily implemented on most operating systems. FTP's versatility also comes from its ability to support various file operations, such as listing directories, renaming files, deleting files, and moving files between directories on the server. These operations make FTP a valuable tool for remote file management and server administration, in addition to file transfer.

Over the years, FTP has become a fundamental protocol in the world of networking, providing a standardized method for transferring files across diverse systems and platforms. Its widespread use in industries such as web development, system administration, and data management has cemented its place as a reliable tool for transferring large amounts of data. While more secure alternatives exist, FTP continues to play an important role in certain contexts where security is not a primary concern, and the primary objective is fast and efficient file transfer. As technology continues to evolve, FTP's simplicity and flexibility ensure that it remains a core part of the network administration toolbox.

The Security Considerations of TFTP

The Trivial File Transfer Protocol (TFTP) is a lightweight, simple protocol primarily used for transferring small files over a network. Although TFTP offers a convenient and efficient method for file transfer, its lack of built-in security features makes it a less desirable option in environments where confidentiality, integrity, and authentication are crucial. TFTP operates over the User Datagram Protocol (UDP), which does not provide the reliability and security features found in other transport protocols like TCP. As a result, understanding the security considerations of TFTP is essential for administrators to assess when and how to use it effectively while mitigating potential security risks.

One of the most significant security concerns with TFTP is the lack of encryption. TFTP does not provide any form of encryption for the data being transmitted, meaning that files transferred via TFTP are sent in clear text across the network. This makes it relatively easy for malicious actors to intercept and capture the data during transmission. Anyone with access to the network can potentially capture the contents of the files being transferred, including sensitive information, such as configuration files or firmware updates. This vulnerability to man-in-the-middle attacks is particularly concerning in untrusted or open networks, where the risk of interception is high.

In addition to the lack of encryption, TFTP does not provide any form of authentication. TFTP does not require users or devices to authenticate themselves before initiating file transfers, which means that anyone who can access the TFTP server or network can request files or send files to the server. This opens the door for unauthorized users to potentially access or upload malicious files to the server, leading to further security risks. Without authentication, there is no way to verify the identity of the client or the server, making it impossible to ensure that the file transfer is legitimate and not being manipulated by a malicious actor.

Another key security consideration with TFTP is its lack of data integrity checks. TFTP does not include any mechanisms for verifying whether the file being transferred is the same as the original, or if it has been corrupted or altered during transmission. This means that TFTP cannot detect if a file has been tampered with in transit, which is a critical vulnerability in situations where the integrity of the data being transferred is important. In the event of network instability or an attempted attack, TFTP transfers may result in corrupted files being received by the client without any indication that the transfer was unsuccessful or compromised. In more secure protocols, such as FTP or SFTP, checksums and other error detection mechanisms are built in to ensure that the data is transmitted accurately and remains intact.

Furthermore, TFTP lacks the ability to restrict or control access to specific files or directories on the server. In many cases, TFTP servers are configured to allow clients to request any file from a specific directory, and there is no native access control mechanism to limit which files can be transferred. This is problematic in situations where sensitive files, such as network configuration files, are stored on the TFTP server. Without the ability to enforce access control policies, unauthorized users may gain access to files that they should not be able to retrieve, potentially leading to information leakage or network misconfigurations.

TFTP also has limited logging capabilities, making it difficult to track and audit file transfers. Most TFTP servers do not have robust logging features, meaning that administrators have little visibility into who accessed the server or which files were transferred. This lack of logging makes it challenging to detect unauthorized activity or troubleshoot issues related to file transfers. In a more secure environment, where logs are essential for monitoring and auditing purposes, TFTP's minimal logging capability represents a serious limitation. Without logs, administrators have no way of knowing if a security breach occurred, or if files were uploaded or downloaded by malicious actors.

One of the other significant security vulnerabilities of TFTP is its use of the User Datagram Protocol (UDP). Unlike Transmission Control Protocol (TCP), which is connection-oriented and ensures reliable delivery of data, UDP is connectionless and does not guarantee that data packets will be delivered correctly or in the proper order. This lack of reliability means that TFTP transfers are more prone to errors and packet loss. While TFTP has its own error recovery mechanisms, they are relatively primitive compared to the more sophisticated mechanisms available in other file transfer protocols. UDP's inherent lack of error correction also makes TFTP more susceptible to denial-of-service (DoS) attacks, where an attacker floods the server with excessive requests, potentially overwhelming it and causing a disruption in service.

Given these security vulnerabilities, TFTP is generally recommended for use only in trusted, isolated networks where security is not a primary concern. For example, TFTP may be appropriate in environments like embedded systems, where devices need to load configuration files or firmware updates, and the network is highly controlled. In these cases, the lack of encryption and authentication is less of a concern because the devices involved are physically secure and isolated from external threats. However, when dealing with sensitive data or transferring files over open or untrusted networks, TFTP is not an ideal choice due to its lack of security features.

To mitigate the security risks associated with TFTP, administrators can implement various countermeasures. One approach is to use TFTP in conjunction with virtual private networks (VPNs) or other secure tunneling protocols. By encrypting the entire network communication, including the TFTP file transfers, VPNs can provide an additional layer of protection against eavesdropping and man-in-the-middle attacks. However, while this may offer some protection, it does not address the core vulnerabilities of TFTP, such as the lack of authentication or data integrity checks. A more secure alternative would be to use a protocol like Secure File Transfer Protocol (SFTP) or File Transfer Protocol Secure (FTPS), which add encryption and authentication to the file transfer process, making them much more suitable for sensitive environments.

Another way to improve the security of TFTP is by restricting access to the TFTP server through firewalls and network segmentation. By ensuring that only authorized clients can access the TFTP server, administrators can reduce the risk of unauthorized access and file manipulation. Implementing access control lists (ACLs) to limit which clients can connect to the server and specifying which files or directories can be accessed can help to mitigate some of the inherent security risks of TFTP. However, these measures are still not as secure as using a more robust file transfer protocol with built-in encryption and authentication features.

In summary, while TFTP is a useful protocol for certain applications, its lack of encryption, authentication, data integrity checks, access controls, and logging makes it unsuitable for use in environments where security is a concern. Administrators must carefully assess the security risks before deploying TFTP and consider employing additional security measures, such as VPNs, firewalls, or more secure protocols like SFTP or FTPS, to protect the integrity and confidentiality of the data being transferred. By understanding these security considerations, network administrators can make informed decisions about when and where to use TFTP, ensuring that its limitations are adequately addressed.

FTP Protocol Structure: An In-Depth Look

The File Transfer Protocol (FTP) is one of the foundational protocols in networking, primarily designed to facilitate the transfer of files between a client and a server. It operates over the Internet Protocol Suite and is commonly used to upload and download files from remote systems, manage files on servers, and support the exchange of documents and data across networks. To understand how FTP works at a deeper level, it is important to examine its structure, which consists of several key components, including the command and data channels, the types of connections it makes, and how data is transferred and managed during the session. The structure of FTP is both simple and highly functional, enabling it to remain a widely-used protocol for file transfers across the world.

FTP uses a client-server architecture, which involves a client initiating a connection to the server and requesting file transfers. At the core of FTP's structure are two communication channels: the control channel and the data channel. These two channels work in tandem to ensure that the file transfer process is efficient and reliable. The control channel, which is typically assigned to port 21, is used for sending commands from the client to the server and for receiving responses back from the server. This channel is responsible for managing the session, including user authentication, file requests, and error handling. The data channel, on the other hand, is used for the actual transfer of files between the client and the server. This channel can use various port numbers, depending on the mode of operation, and is responsible for transmitting the file content.

When a client connects to the FTP server, it first establishes a control connection over the TCP/IP network. The client sends a request to the server to begin the session, and the server responds with a status message indicating whether the connection was successful and whether the client has been authenticated. After authentication, the client and server communicate over the control channel to exchange various commands and responses. These commands can include simple actions like changing directories on the server, listing files in a directory, or transferring files to and from the server. Each command issued by the client is followed by a response from the server, which confirms the success or failure of the operation and provides additional information, such as error codes or transfer statuses.

The data channel is where the actual file transfer takes place. Unlike the control channel, which is kept open throughout the session, the data channel is established separately each time a file transfer is requested. This channel is used to transfer the actual file content, whether it is being uploaded to or downloaded from the server. The data channel is typically initiated by the server, but FTP supports both active and passive modes, which affect how the data channel is created and maintained during the session.

In active mode, the client establishes a connection to the server's control port, typically port 21, and the server then opens a separate random port to transfer the data. The client listens for a connection on its own random port, and once this is set up, the server can initiate the data transfer. In this scenario, the server controls the connection and sends the file directly to the client's data port. The downside of this setup is that firewalls or network address translation (NAT) devices often block incoming connections to the client's data port, making active mode unsuitable for many modern networks.

In contrast, passive mode reverses the process to accommodate situations where the client is behind a firewall or NAT device. In passive mode, the client establishes the control connection with the server, but instead of the server opening a random port for the data connection, the server listens on a random port for the data transfer.

The server sends this port number back to the client over the control channel, and the client initiates the data connection by connecting to the server's data port. Passive mode resolves the firewall and NAT issues that occur in active mode, making it more suitable for many modern applications.

FTP transfers files in two different modes: ASCII mode and binary mode. The mode selected determines how the file is transmitted over the data channel. In ASCII mode, text files are transferred as plain text, with the protocol taking care to ensure that line endings are properly converted between different operating systems, such as Windows, UNIX, or macOS. This mode is useful for transferring text files, such as configuration files, scripts, or documents, that do not contain binary data. On the other hand, binary mode is used for files that contain non-text data, such as images, videos, and executables. In binary mode, the file is transferred exactly as it is, byte for byte, without any alterations to the data. This ensures that binary files are transferred intact and without corruption, which would be a concern in ASCII mode due to the way character encoding and line endings are handled.

One of the fundamental aspects of FTP's structure is its reliance on well-defined commands and responses. The FTP client sends commands to the server to request specific actions, such as retrieving a file, storing a file, or changing directories. Each command is associated with a numeric code, which helps identify the result of the request. The server responds with a numeric status code, followed by an optional text message that provides more detailed information. These status codes are categorized into groups based on the type of response. For example, a code beginning with "2" indicates a successful action, while codes starting with "4" or "5" indicate error conditions.

Some common FTP commands include USER and PASS for authentication, RETR for retrieving files, STOR for storing files, and LIST for listing files in a directory. These commands are straightforward but enable the client to interact with the server in a flexible way. FTP also supports more complex operations such as changing file permissions, deleting files, and renaming files on the server, providing comprehensive file management capabilities beyond simple file transfers.

Despite its long history and widespread use, FTP has significant limitations, particularly in terms of security. FTP does not encrypt the data transferred between the client and the server, meaning that all information, including sensitive data such as usernames, passwords, and file contents, is transmitted in plaintext. This makes FTP highly vulnerable to interception and man-in-the-middle attacks. For this reason, FTP is often used in environments where security is not a critical concern, or when additional security measures, such as VPNs or firewalls, are used to protect the communication.

To address these security concerns, several more secure variants of FTP have been developed, including FTPS and SFTP. FTPS extends FTP by adding support for SSL/TLS encryption to secure the control and data channels, providing confidentiality and integrity for file transfers. SFTP, or Secure File Transfer Protocol, is a completely different protocol based on SSH (Secure Shell) that provides a secure alternative to FTP by encrypting both the control and data channels. These secure versions of FTP are commonly used in modern networks to protect the confidentiality of sensitive data.

While FTP is now often supplanted by its more secure variants, its simple, robust structure continues to make it a useful tool for certain file transfer tasks. The protocol's two-channel communication model, the different operational modes, and its command-response structure all contribute to its ongoing utility in environments where high security is not a primary concern but where efficient, reliable file transfers are needed. As networks evolve and the need for secure, high-performance file transfer solutions increases, FTP's role in modern network communication is supplemented by more secure alternatives, but its foundational principles remain a cornerstone of file transfer technology.

Configuring TFTP on Network Devices

The Trivial File Transfer Protocol (TFTP) is widely used in networking for transferring files, especially configuration files and firmware updates, between network devices. Despite its simplicity, TFTP remains an essential tool for network administrators, particularly in environments where ease of implementation and speed are prioritized over security. Configuring TFTP on network devices involves a series of steps that allow network administrators to set up TFTP servers and ensure proper communication between devices for transferring files. While TFTP's minimalistic design makes it easy to deploy, it also requires careful consideration of network topology and security.

To begin configuring TFTP on network devices, administrators must first ensure that a TFTP server is available. A TFTP server is a software application that runs on a computer or server, allowing it to listen for file transfer requests from TFTP clients. These servers are often configured to allow devices within a specific network or subnet to upload or download files, such as firmware images, configuration files, and system backups. Popular TFTP server software includes applications like SolarWinds TFTP Server, PumpKIN, and OpenTFTP, which can be easily installed and configured on a server within the network.

Once the TFTP server is set up and running, the next step involves configuring the network devices to interact with the TFTP server. Network devices such as routers, switches, and firewalls often need to be configured to point to the correct TFTP server address. This typically involves accessing the device's configuration interface, usually through a command-line interface (CLI) or a web-based graphical user interface (GUI), depending on the device. The device must be configured with the IP address of the TFTP server, so it knows where to send or receive the files.

On most network devices, the TFTP configuration is relatively straightforward. For instance, in Cisco network devices, administrators would access the global configuration mode and enter commands to set the TFTP server IP address and initiate file transfers. The copy command is used to instruct the device to transfer files from or to the TFTP server. For example, the command copy tftp: running-config can be used to copy the running configuration of the device to the TFTP server, while copy running-config tftp: allows the device to download a configuration file from the server.

After configuring the network device with the TFTP server's IP address, administrators must ensure that the network allows TFTP traffic to flow between the device and the server. TFTP operates over UDP port 69 by default, and it is essential to check that firewalls or access control lists (ACLs) are configured to allow traffic on this port. If the network device or TFTP server is protected by a firewall, the firewall must be configured to permit incoming and outgoing TFTP traffic. Additionally, because TFTP does not encrypt its data, ensuring that the device and server are within a secure and trusted network is important for minimizing the risks of interception or data tampering.

Once the basic configuration is complete, the device and the TFTP server are ready for file transfers. TFTP can be used for a variety of tasks, such as backing up configuration files, updating firmware, or restoring device configurations. For example, administrators can use TFTP to back up a router's configuration file to a TFTP server by issuing the appropriate command in the router's CLI. Similarly, TFTP can be used to upload a new firmware image to a device, allowing administrators to upgrade or restore the device's operating system quickly. The process is often automated, with scheduled backups set up to ensure that configuration files are regularly copied to a secure location.

Another common use of TFTP in network device configuration is for loading boot images. Many network devices, such as routers and switches, use TFTP during the boot process to download firmware or operating system images from a TFTP server. This is particularly useful in situations where devices need to be quickly reconfigured or reimaged after a failure or software corruption. By configuring the device to use TFTP as a boot source, administrators can remotely recover devices without needing to physically access them, saving time and effort in disaster recovery scenarios.

While configuring TFTP on network devices is relatively simple, administrators should also consider the security implications of using the protocol. TFTP does not provide encryption or authentication, making it vulnerable to a variety of attacks, including man-in-the-middle and denial-of-service attacks. As TFTP transfers files in plain text, it is crucial that it is only used within trusted networks. In environments where security is a higher priority, it is recommended to use a more secure protocol, such as SFTP or FTPS, which offer encryption and authentication features to protect the integrity and confidentiality of the files being transferred.

For environments where TFTP is necessary, administrators can implement certain measures to mitigate the risks associated with the protocol. For instance, using a dedicated VLAN or isolated network for TFTP communications can help limit exposure to potential threats. Additionally, restricting access to the TFTP server by configuring ACLs on the server or network devices can help prevent unauthorized access. By allowing only specific IP addresses or subnets to communicate with the TFTP server, administrators can reduce the risk of unauthorized file transfers.

One of the main advantages of TFTP is its simplicity, which makes it easy to deploy and use, even in complex networks. However, this simplicity also means that it lacks many of the features found in more advanced file transfer protocols, such as encryption, user authentication, and error recovery. Administrators must therefore be cautious about where and how TFTP is used, ensuring that it is limited to scenarios where security concerns are minimal, and the benefits of speed and simplicity outweigh the risks.

In large-scale networks, managing TFTP servers and devices can become more complex. In such environments, administrators may need to implement centralized management tools or automated processes to handle multiple devices and ensure consistency across the network. These tools can help manage TFTP file transfers, back up configurations regularly, and automate firmware updates, reducing the administrative workload and minimizing the potential for errors.

To further streamline TFTP management, network administrators can use scripts or automation frameworks to initiate scheduled transfers or configure multiple devices simultaneously. For example, an automation script might be created to back up the configuration of all routers and switches in the network at a specific time every day, ensuring that the most recent configurations are always available in case of a failure. This level of automation not only improves efficiency but also reduces the chances of human error during critical tasks such as configuration backups or firmware updates.

Configuring TFTP on network devices requires careful planning and attention to detail to ensure that the protocol functions as intended while minimizing security risks. By setting up a secure TFTP environment, using firewalls and ACLs to restrict access, and automating file transfers where possible, administrators can leverage TFTP's simplicity and speed to manage network devices effectively. While TFTP may not be suitable for all use cases due to its lack of security features, it remains a valuable tool for file transfer in controlled and trusted network environments.

Troubleshooting TFTP Operations

Trivial File Transfer Protocol (TFTP) is a simple and lightweight protocol used for transferring files across a network, but like any network protocol, it can experience issues that prevent successful file transfers. As TFTP is widely used for tasks such as backing up device configurations, uploading firmware, and recovering systems, it is essential for network administrators to be able to diagnose and resolve any issues that may arise during its operation. Troubleshooting TFTP requires a structured approach to identify the source of the problem, as TFTP operates with minimal error handling and does not provide much feedback when something goes wrong. Understanding how to troubleshoot TFTP operations involves exploring common issues, identifying potential causes, and applying solutions to restore functionality.

One of the most common issues administrators encounter when working with TFTP is connection failure between the client and the server. TFTP relies on UDP port 69 for communication, and if there are any issues with the network connection or firewall settings, the TFTP client may fail to establish a connection with the TFTP server. A failure to connect can occur if the server is not reachable, either due to incorrect IP address configuration or network segmentation issues. The first step in troubleshooting such a problem is to verify that the TFTP server is operational and correctly configured. Administrators should check the server's IP address, ensure that the TFTP service is running, and verify that the server is accessible from the client's network.

One way to test the server's availability is to perform a basic ping test. By pinging the server from the client's machine, administrators can determine whether there is basic network connectivity. If the ping test fails, it indicates a more fundamental network issue, such as a misconfigured network interface, incorrect IP address, or a routing problem. In such cases, network administrators should review the network configuration and ensure that both the client and the server are within the same subnet or can communicate across routers if necessary. If the ping test is successful but TFTP still fails to connect, the issue may lie in firewall configurations. Firewalls can block UDP traffic on port 69, preventing the client from communicating with the TFTP server.

To address firewall issues, administrators need to ensure that both the client and the server's firewall settings allow UDP traffic on port 69. This may involve configuring the firewall to permit inbound and outbound TFTP traffic. On servers, network administrators may need to adjust access control lists (ACLs) or rules in firewall software to allow the TFTP service to pass through. If the client or server is behind a firewall or Network Address Translation (NAT) device, it may also be necessary to configure the firewall or NAT to forward the relevant ports correctly. If using active mode for TFTP, the client must allow incoming UDP connections from the server's randomly assigned data ports, which is another aspect to consider when troubleshooting TFTP connectivity.

Another common issue in TFTP operations is failure to transfer files. This can manifest in various ways, such as the client receiving incomplete files or no files at all. Several factors can contribute to this problem. First, administrators should check that the TFTP server has the correct permissions set to allow read and write access to the directories from which it serves files. If the server is unable to read or write to its directory due to permission issues, file transfers will fail. On many servers, files are served from specific directories, and incorrect permissions on these directories can result in failure to transfer files to or from the server.

File size limitations can also affect TFTP file transfers. TFTP typically operates with a 16-bit block size, meaning that it can only handle transfers of files up to 32 MB in size. Larger files will fail to transfer, and administrators should verify that the file size does not exceed the protocol's limitations. In such cases, administrators may need to consider using an alternative protocol, such as FTP, SFTP, or SCP, which are better suited for transferring larger files.

Another issue that can affect TFTP transfers is network instability. TFTP operates over UDP, a connectionless protocol, meaning that it does not have built-in mechanisms to ensure the reliability of data transmission. If the network experiences high levels of congestion, packet loss, or other issues that affect the UDP traffic, file transfers may fail. Administrators can use network monitoring tools to check for issues such as high latency or packet loss that may be affecting TFTP performance. If network instability is detected, resolving the underlying network issues, such as upgrading hardware, optimizing routing, or reducing congestion, may be necessary to restore reliable TFTP operations.

If TFTP transfers are slow, the issue may lie in network bandwidth or hardware limitations. TFTP is designed to be lightweight and efficient, but if either the client or the server has insufficient processing power or bandwidth to handle the file transfer, the process may be delayed. Administrators should monitor CPU and network utilization on both the TFTP server and client to ensure that neither device is being overwhelmed during the transfer. If bandwidth is a limiting factor, it may be necessary to upgrade the network infrastructure or schedule file transfers during off-peak hours to reduce congestion.

Another potential problem that can occur when using TFTP is the corruption of the files being transferred. Since TFTP does not provide data integrity checks, it is possible for files to become corrupted during the transfer process, especially if there are network errors or the file is too large for the protocol to handle properly. In some cases, TFTP clients or servers may have an option to verify file integrity after a transfer, but this is not a built-in feature of the protocol itself. To prevent corruption, administrators should ensure that the network is stable and reliable and consider using more secure protocols for transferring critical files, such as SFTP or FTPS, which provide built-in error checking and encryption.

In some cases, the issue may be related to the configuration settings on the TFTP client or server. For example, some TFTP clients require a specific format for file paths, while others may have restrictions on the type of file transfers they can handle. It is important to review both the server's and client's configuration settings to ensure that they are compatible with each other. Misconfigured options, such as incorrect directory paths, file names, or permissions, can result in TFTP transfer failures.

Administrators should also be aware of issues related to TFTP server software. Some servers may have bugs or incompatibilities with certain operating systems or network configurations, leading to intermittent failures or unpredictable behavior. In such cases, updating the TFTP server software to the latest version may resolve the problem. Additionally, using an alternative TFTP server software package may provide better reliability or performance for certain environments.

When troubleshooting TFTP operations, a methodical approach is key. Starting with basic checks like network connectivity, verifying permissions, and ensuring proper firewall settings can help isolate the cause of the issue. Monitoring network stability and ensuring that file sizes are within the protocol's limits are also important steps. Once these common issues are ruled out, more advanced checks, such as reviewing configuration settings or updating software, can further narrow down the source of the problem. By systematically addressing each potential issue, network administrators can restore normal TFTP operations and ensure that file transfers occur reliably and efficiently.

Benefits and Limitations of TFTP in Network Management

The Trivial File Transfer Protocol (TFTP) has long been a staple of network management due to its simplicity and ease of use. It is often chosen for tasks that require quick and efficient file transfers between network devices, such as routers, switches, and servers. TFTP is especially beneficial in environments where file size is small, security concerns are minimal, and the need for advanced features like encryption and authentication is not a priority. Despite its advantages, TFTP also comes with several limitations that can make it unsuitable for more demanding or security-conscious network environments. A thorough understanding of the benefits and limitations of TFTP is crucial for network administrators to decide when and where to use the protocol effectively.

One of the primary benefits of TFTP is its simplicity. The protocol is designed to be lightweight, requiring minimal configuration and no complex setup. This simplicity makes it an attractive choice for network administrators who need a quick, no-fuss solution for transferring files. The basic structure of TFTP means that it does not require the overhead of connection establishment or error-checking mechanisms found in more complex protocols like FTP or SFTP. This lightweight design allows TFTP to operate quickly, even on devices with limited processing power, such as embedded systems or network appliances. When network administrators need to perform tasks such as transferring firmware, configuration files, or diagnostic data, TFTP provides a streamlined, straightforward solution.

Another key benefit of TFTP is its speed. Due to the protocol's simplicity, there is minimal overhead involved in establishing a connection and transferring data. TFTP operates over UDP (User Datagram Protocol), which is a connectionless protocol. Unlike TCP, which requires a connection to be established before data transfer begins, UDP sends data without the need for handshakes or acknowledgment of receipt. This makes TFTP an ideal choice for situations where speed is more important than reliability or where the files being transferred are small and can be easily retried if necessary. This makes TFTP particularly well-suited for environments where network devices need to be quickly configured or updated with minimal delay.

In addition to speed and simplicity, TFTP is also beneficial in environments with limited resources. Many network devices, such as routers, switches, and firewalls, have constrained processing power and memory. TFTP's lightweight design allows it to operate effectively on these devices without overwhelming their limited resources. Devices that use TFTP for tasks like firmware upgrades or configuration backups can perform these functions without significant impact on their overall performance. This is an important consideration in large-scale networks, where minimizing resource consumption is essential for maintaining optimal network performance.

TFTP's low resource requirements and speed also make it a useful tool for automated processes. For example, network administrators can automate tasks like regularly backing up configuration files or updating device firmware without the need for manual intervention. Because TFTP is so simple, it can be easily integrated into network automation scripts or management systems. These automated processes save time and reduce the likelihood of human error, ensuring that configurations and firmware updates are performed consistently and on schedule. This makes TFTP an essential tool in the toolkit of administrators who manage large numbers of network devices.

Despite its numerous benefits, TFTP does have several limitations that must be considered when deciding whether it is the right protocol for a given task. One of the most significant limitations of TFTP is its lack of security features. TFTP does not offer encryption, authentication, or access control, meaning that files transferred using the protocol are sent in clear text. This makes TFTP inherently insecure for transferring sensitive information, such as passwords, private keys, or confidential configuration data. In untrusted networks, or in situations where the data being transferred is critical, TFTP is not an appropriate choice. For secure file transfers, network administrators typically turn to protocols like SFTP or FTPS, which provide the necessary encryption and authentication to protect sensitive data.

The absence of encryption in TFTP also exposes it to the risk of man-in-the-middle attacks. Since TFTP sends data unencrypted, an attacker who gains access to the network could potentially intercept and modify the files being transferred. This poses a significant risk, particularly in open or public networks, where unauthorized access is more likely. For sensitive applications, where the integrity of the transferred data is paramount, TFTP is unsuitable. Even in trusted, isolated environments, the lack of encryption can still be problematic, as it exposes the data to potential tampering or eavesdropping.

Another limitation of TFTP is its lack of error recovery and data integrity mechanisms. Because TFTP operates over UDP, it does not include built-in mechanisms for ensuring that data is delivered reliably. UDP does not acknowledge the receipt of packets, meaning that if data is lost or corrupted during transmission, there is no automatic way for the protocol to detect or correct the problem. If a file transfer is interrupted or if network conditions cause packet loss, the client and server may not realize that the transfer was incomplete or corrupted. As a result, administrators must manually check for errors or incomplete transfers, which can be time-consuming and error-prone. In contrast, more sophisticated protocols like FTP or SCP automatically handle errors and ensure the integrity of the transferred data through mechanisms such as checksums and retries.

TFTP's inability to handle large files is another limitation that can make it less suitable for certain tasks. TFTP was designed with simplicity in mind and, as a result, it supports only relatively small file transfers. The protocol operates with a 16-bit block size, which limits the maximum file size to 32 MB. While this may be sufficient for many network management tasks, such as configuration backups and firmware updates, it becomes a significant limitation when transferring larger files. For files that exceed this size, TFTP is not an appropriate choice. In such cases, network administrators may need to resort to other file transfer protocols, such as FTP or SCP, which support larger file sizes and provide more robust error handling.

The lack of file management features is another drawback of TFTP. TFTP is a basic file transfer protocol that allows files to be transferred between a client and server, but it does not include features for managing files on the server. Unlike more advanced protocols like FTP, TFTP does not support directory listings, file renaming, or file manipulation. This makes TFTP unsuitable for tasks that require more advanced file management capabilities. For example, if a network administrator needs to move or rename a file on the server before transferring it, TFTP cannot perform this operation. Instead, the administrator must manually manage the files on the server outside of the TFTP protocol.

Despite these limitations, TFTP remains an important tool in network management, especially in environments where security concerns are minimal, file sizes are small, and speed and simplicity are prioritized. It is particularly useful for tasks like firmware updates, configuration backups, and file transfers between embedded systems or network devices with limited processing power. However, for tasks that involve large file transfers, sensitive data, or more complex file management needs, administrators must consider alternative protocols that offer stronger security, reliability, and error handling capabilities. Understanding both the benefits and limitations of TFTP allows network administrators to use the protocol effectively and make informed decisions about when it is appropriate to deploy in their network environments.

The Importance of SCP in Configuration Management

The Secure Copy Protocol (SCP) plays a crucial role in the realm of configuration management by providing a secure and reliable method for transferring configuration files between systems. Unlike older, less secure protocols like TFTP, SCP ensures that data transferred between a client and a server is encrypted and protected against interception. This security feature makes SCP particularly valuable in today's network environments, where sensitive data and critical configurations need to be handled with the utmost care. As the complexity of network infrastructures grows, SCP has become an essential tool for administrators who must maintain consistent configurations across numerous devices while safeguarding against security vulnerabilities. The importance of SCP in configuration management cannot be overstated, particularly as businesses and organizations increasingly rely on secure, efficient methods for managing and transferring configuration files.

One of the primary reasons SCP is vital to configuration management is its ability to provide strong encryption for file transfers. Network devices, such as routers, switches, firewalls, and servers, often require regular updates to their configurations to ensure that they operate effectively and securely. These configurations may include sensitive information, such as IP addresses, access control lists, and firewall settings. Without encryption, this information could be intercepted during transmission, exposing networks to potential security breaches. SCP addresses this concern by leveraging the Secure Shell (SSH) protocol, which encrypts both the control and data channels during file transfer. This encryption ensures that the integrity and confidentiality of the configuration files are maintained, protecting the sensitive information from being exposed to unauthorized parties.

The use of SCP in configuration management is particularly important for organizations that manage large-scale, distributed networks. These networks may consist of hundreds or even thousands of devices, each requiring specific configurations that must be regularly updated and maintained. Manually managing the configurations of these devices can be an arduous and error-prone task, especially when using unsecured protocols. SCP, however, provides a streamlined and secure method for administrators to transfer configuration files to and from network devices with minimal effort. Whether it is for backing up configurations, uploading new settings, or restoring a device to a previous configuration, SCP ensures that the process is both efficient and secure.

Furthermore, SCP offers a high degree of automation, which is a crucial factor in modern network management. Many network administrators automate routine configuration management tasks, such as regularly backing up device configurations or pushing updates to multiple devices at once. SCP plays a critical role in this automation by providing a reliable and secure method for transferring files between devices and centralized configuration management systems. For example, an administrator can write a script to automatically back up the configurations of multiple routers and switches on a scheduled basis, ensuring that the most recent configuration is always available for recovery in case of a failure. With SCP, these tasks can be performed with minimal human intervention, significantly reducing the risk of manual errors and improving the overall efficiency of network management operations.

SCP also simplifies the process of configuration management in remote or distributed environments. Many network devices are located in remote locations or are part of distributed systems that require regular configuration updates. Traditional methods of transferring

40

configuration files, such as using physical storage devices or relying on less secure protocols, can be cumbersome and inefficient. SCP eliminates these challenges by allowing administrators to securely transfer files over the internet or any other network connection. This capability is particularly beneficial for organizations with branch offices, remote sites, or cloud-based infrastructure, where devices may be located far from the central management console. With SCP, administrators can securely manage and update configurations from anywhere, ensuring that their network devices are always running the correct settings and remain compliant with security policies.

Another significant advantage of SCP is its ability to facilitate efficient backup and recovery processes. In any network environment, the ability to quickly restore a device to a known working configuration is critical for minimizing downtime and reducing the impact of failures or misconfigurations. SCP allows administrators to securely back up device configurations to centralized servers, ensuring that copies of the most recent configurations are readily available. If a device fails or needs to be reset, administrators can quickly restore the device's configuration using the SCP protocol, minimizing downtime and preventing the loss of critical settings. Additionally, SCP's use of SSH for secure authentication ensures that only authorized administrators can access and transfer configuration files, further enhancing the security of the backup and recovery process.

In addition to providing security and automation, SCP's role in configuration management extends to its ability to support a wide range of devices and operating systems. SCP is compatible with many different network devices, including those running various versions of UNIX, Linux, and Windows operating systems. This broad compatibility makes SCP an ideal choice for organizations with heterogeneous networks, where devices from different manufacturers and running different operating systems need to be managed. The ability to use a single protocol for transferring configuration files across diverse systems simplifies the overall management process and reduces the complexity associated with using multiple different protocols for different devices.

Despite its many benefits, there are some limitations to SCP that administrators should be aware of when incorporating it into their configuration management practices. One potential limitation is that SCP is primarily designed for file transfers and does not offer the same level of flexibility as other protocols, such as FTP or SFTP, when it comes to file management. For example, SCP does not support operations like directory listings or file renaming, meaning that administrators cannot manipulate files on the remote server as easily as they can with FTP. Additionally, SCP relies on SSH for authentication, which may require more complex setup and configuration compared to other protocols that offer simpler authentication methods. However, these limitations are often outweighed by the security and reliability that SCP provides for transferring configuration files.

Another consideration when using SCP is the fact that it requires SSH to be configured and running on both the client and the server. In some environments, particularly where devices are running older or proprietary operating systems, SSH may not be available or may require additional configuration to enable. While most modern network devices support SSH, administrators may encounter challenges when attempting to implement SCP on legacy equipment or systems that do not have SSH capabilities.

Despite these challenges, the benefits of SCP in configuration management far outweigh its limitations. SCP's ability to securely transfer configuration files, automate processes, and provide a simple yet powerful solution for managing network devices makes it an indispensable tool for network administrators. As the complexity and scale of network environments continue to grow, SCP's role in ensuring the security, consistency, and reliability of network configurations will only become more critical. By leveraging SCP in their configuration management workflows, administrators can ensure that their network devices remain properly configured, secure, and operational, regardless of the size or scope of the network.

Secure Copy Protocol (SCP): Overview and Security Features

The Secure Copy Protocol (SCP) is a network protocol used for securely transferring files between a client and a server, leveraging the security features of the Secure Shell (SSH) protocol. SCP is widely utilized in environments where confidentiality, integrity, and authentication are critical, providing a secure method to transfer sensitive files over an untrusted network, such as the internet. Although SCP shares some similarities with other file transfer protocols like FTP, it distinguishes itself through its focus on security, making it a preferred choice for tasks that require the secure movement of files, such as backing up system configurations, transferring sensitive data, or updating firmware on network devices.

At its core, SCP operates by copying files between a local and a remote system or between two remote systems over a secure connection. Unlike traditional file transfer protocols, such as FTP or TFTP, SCP does not transmit data in plain text. Instead, it relies on SSH to provide encryption for both the authentication process and the file transfer itself. This ensures that all data, including sensitive information like usernames, passwords, and file contents, is protected against eavesdropping and unauthorized access. SCP's primary advantage over other protocols is its inherent security, as it uses SSH for both authentication and encryption, thereby ensuring that the communication remains private and tamper-resistant.

The process of using SCP for file transfers begins with the establishment of an SSH connection between the client and the server. SSH handles the authentication of both the client and the server, ensuring that only authorized users can access the remote system and initiate file transfers. Once the connection is established, SCP allows the client to copy files to or from the server over the encrypted SSH channel. The data being transferred is encrypted during the transmission process, which means that even if the data is intercepted during transfer, it cannot be read or modified by unauthorized entities. This encryption provides an essential layer of protection for the integrity and confidentiality of the data being transferred.

One of the key security features of SCP is its ability to authenticate both the client and the server. Authentication is crucial in any secure communication process, as it verifies the identities of the parties involved in the transfer. SCP uses SSH keys for authentication, which are cryptographic keys that ensure only authorized users can access the system. These keys can either be generated by the user or by a trusted third-party certificate authority, and they provide a much higher level of security compared to traditional password-based authentication. By requiring SSH key-based authentication, SCP eliminates the risk of password theft or brute-force attacks, which are common threats in less secure file transfer protocols.

Another important aspect of SCP's security features is its use of cryptographic hashing algorithms to ensure the integrity of the transferred files. When SCP initiates a file transfer, it computes a hash value for the file, which acts as a unique fingerprint of the file's contents. This hash value is transmitted alongside the file, allowing the receiving system to recompute the hash and verify that the file has not been altered during transmission. If the hash values on the sending and receiving systems do not match, it indicates that the file has been corrupted or tampered with in transit, and the transfer can be stopped before any damage is done. This feature makes SCP an excellent choice for transferring critical files, such as configuration files or software updates, where integrity is paramount.

SCP's security extends beyond encryption and authentication to encompass the protection of the entire file transfer process. The protocol prevents unauthorized access by restricting the ability to initiate file transfers to users who have valid SSH credentials. Unlike less secure protocols, SCP ensures that only authenticated users can upload or download files from the remote server. Additionally, SCP does not provide a mechanism for anonymous file transfers, further reducing the risk of unauthorized access. This level of access control is essential for organizations that need to ensure that only specific individuals or systems can interact with sensitive files.

One of the significant benefits of SCP is that it works seamlessly in a wide range of environments, from small networks to large-scale enterprise infrastructures. SCP can be used to transfer files between systems running different operating systems, such as UNIX, Linux, and

Windows. The compatibility of SCP across various platforms makes it a versatile tool for network administrators, who can rely on it to securely manage files and configurations across different types of devices and operating systems. The ability to use SCP for both local and remote file transfers makes it especially useful for managing distributed systems, where network devices and servers are spread across multiple locations.

SCP also provides a fast and efficient means of transferring files, thanks to its simple and lightweight design. Unlike more complex protocols, SCP does not require an extensive setup process or a large number of configuration options. The simplicity of SCP makes it a reliable and quick tool for transferring files in situations where speed is important, such as during firmware updates or emergency configuration changes. Although it does not have as many advanced features as FTP or SFTP, SCP's focus on security and simplicity makes it a strong contender for specific use cases where security is the primary concern.

Despite its numerous advantages, SCP does have some limitations. One of the main drawbacks of SCP is that it is not as flexible as other file transfer protocols, such as SFTP or FTP. SCP is primarily designed for transferring files between systems, but it lacks the features required for more complex file management tasks. For example, SCP does not support operations such as directory listing, file renaming, or file deletion, making it less suitable for environments where file manipulation is required. This limitation makes SCP better suited for simple file transfers rather than full-scale file management.

Additionally, while SCP is highly secure, its reliance on SSH for encryption and authentication can make it difficult to set up and manage in certain environments. SSH requires the configuration of keys and permissions, which can be complex for administrators who are not familiar with the process. Furthermore, SSH's reliance on keys rather than passwords can lead to challenges in managing and rotating keys, especially in large environments where many systems and users are involved. These factors can make SCP less user-friendly compared to simpler protocols that rely on password-based authentication.

Despite these limitations, SCP remains an essential tool for securely transferring files in network environments. Its ability to provide encrypted file transfers, strong authentication, and file integrity checks makes it a valuable asset for network administrators who need to safeguard sensitive data. Whether it is used for routine configuration backups, software updates, or transferring critical files across an untrusted network, SCP ensures that the integrity and confidentiality of the data are preserved throughout the transfer process. By using SCP, organizations can effectively manage their network devices and configurations while minimizing the risk of security breaches and data theft. The protocol's security features, simplicity, and compatibility make it a reliable choice for file transfer in environments where protecting data is of paramount importance.

SCP Protocol Structure and Operations

The Secure Copy Protocol (SCP) is an integral part of modern network administration, offering a secure method for transferring files between systems over a network. SCP is based on the Secure Shell (SSH) protocol and provides encryption for both the authentication and data transfer phases. This ensures that file transfers are protected from interception and unauthorized access, making SCP a preferred choice for managing configuration files, backup data, and other sensitive information in network environments. To fully understand SCP's functionality, it is essential to explore its protocol structure and the operations involved in the file transfer process. By examining these components, one can appreciate the role SCP plays in securing network communications and data exchanges.

SCP operates in a client-server model, with the client initiating the connection and the server responding to the client's requests. Both the client and the server must have SSH set up and running in order to use SCP. This reliance on SSH ensures that all communications between the client and the server are encrypted and authenticated. The protocol is designed to copy files securely between systems, and while it shares similarities with other file transfer protocols, such as FTP or TFTP, its key differentiator lies in its security. SCP ensures that files are encrypted during transit, preventing eavesdropping or unauthorized access. Additionally, the use of SSH for authentication means that only authorized users with valid SSH keys or credentials can access the remote server and perform file transfers.

The structure of SCP is relatively simple compared to other file transfer protocols. At its core, SCP is designed to facilitate the secure transfer of files from one system to another. The protocol operates over a single encrypted SSH connection, which is used for both authentication and file transfer. The first step in using SCP is establishing an SSH connection between the client and the server. This connection is used for the exchange of authentication information, such as SSH keys or passwords, ensuring that both parties are authorized to communicate with each other. Once the SSH connection is established and the authentication is complete, the actual file transfer process can begin.

SCP uses a command-line interface to initiate file transfers. A user on the client system will typically issue a command specifying the source and destination files. The command includes the path to the file on the client system and the path where it should be copied on the server, as well as the IP address or hostname of the server. For example, the command may look something like this: scp file.txt user@hostname:/path/to/destination. This tells the SCP client to copy file.txt from the local system to the specified directory on the remote system. The client uses the SSH protocol to securely transmit the file over the network.

Once the file transfer request is made, SCP proceeds with the operation by using the underlying SSH connection to transfer the data in encrypted form. The encryption ensures that even if the file transfer is intercepted while in transit, the data remains unreadable to unauthorized parties. SCP does not support many of the advanced features found in other file transfer protocols like FTP. For example, SCP does not provide the ability to list directories or perform complex file operations, such as renaming or deleting files on the server. Instead, SCP is streamlined for the primary purpose of securely copying files between systems. This simplicity is one of the reasons why it is often chosen for configuration management tasks, where quick, secure file transfers are required.

One of the critical operations in SCP is its file integrity check. SCP uses a hashing algorithm to verify the integrity of the files being transferred.

When the file is copied from the client to the server, the source system generates a hash value for the file before it is transmitted. Once the file reaches the destination system, the receiving system recalculates the hash of the incoming file. If the calculated hash on both the client and server matches, it indicates that the file has been transferred successfully without any corruption. This feature is particularly useful in network environments where data integrity is vital, as it ensures that no modifications or errors have occurred during the transfer.

SCP also provides robust authentication features, primarily through SSH key-based authentication. This type of authentication is more secure than traditional password-based authentication, as it uses a pair of cryptographic keys to verify the identity of the client and the server. The private key is stored on the client machine, and the public key is placed on the server. When the client tries to connect, the server sends a challenge to the client that can only be answered correctly using the private key. If the client provides the correct response, the server grants access and initiates the file transfer. This method of authentication is resistant to brute-force attacks and provides a higher level of security than using passwords.

The SCP protocol also benefits from its compatibility with different operating systems. SCP can be used to transfer files between machines running different versions of UNIX, Linux, and even Windows, as long as SSH is enabled. This cross-platform compatibility makes SCP an ideal tool for network administrators who need to manage configurations and files across a diverse set of systems. Whether transferring files from a Linux server to a Windows workstation or between two UNIX systems, SCP ensures that the process remains secure and efficient.

Despite its strengths, SCP does have limitations that should be considered when deciding whether to use it for a given task. While it excels in security and simplicity, SCP does not offer advanced file management capabilities. It lacks support for operations like directory listings, file renaming, or remote file manipulation, which are available in more feature-rich protocols like FTP or SFTP. For administrators who need more extensive file management features, SCP may not be the best choice. SCP is also not as user-friendly as other protocols, as it requires familiarity with command-line syntax and SSH key management. For environments where ease of use is a priority, or where a graphical interface is required, SCP may not be the most convenient option.

Furthermore, SCP does not have the ability to resume interrupted transfers. If a file transfer is interrupted due to network issues or server errors, SCP will not automatically resume the transfer from where it left off. This can be an inconvenience when transferring large files, as it requires the entire file to be transferred again from the beginning. For this reason, administrators working with larger files or less stable networks might consider using SFTP, which includes features like resume support and more advanced error handling.

The SCP protocol operates on the same principles as SSH, providing a secure, encrypted method of file transfer that ensures data integrity and confidentiality. Its simplicity, speed, and security make it a valuable tool for many network administration tasks, particularly in the realm of configuration management. SCP's ability to securely transfer files, along with its efficient file integrity checks and strong authentication, ensures that it remains a reliable choice for managing files and configurations in sensitive environments. By understanding its structure and operations, administrators can leverage SCP to streamline their file transfer processes while maintaining high levels of security and efficiency in their networks.

Configuring SCP on Devices for Secure File Transfer

The Secure Copy Protocol (SCP) is a powerful tool for securely transferring files across a network, utilizing the security features of the Secure Shell (SSH) protocol. It is widely used in network environments where encryption and authentication are paramount, such as when transferring configuration files, firmware updates, or sensitive data between devices. Configuring SCP on network devices allows administrators to automate secure file transfers, ensure data integrity, and protect network communications from unauthorized access. The process of configuring SCP on network devices typically involves enabling SSH on the devices, configuring the devices for SCP file transfers, and ensuring that all security measures are in place to protect the transfer process.

The first step in configuring SCP on devices for secure file transfer is enabling SSH on the devices involved. SSH is the underlying protocol that SCP relies on for authentication and encryption, so it must be properly configured and running on both the source and destination devices. In many modern network devices, such as routers, switches, and firewalls, SSH is often disabled by default for security reasons. Administrators need to access the device's command-line interface (CLI) and enable SSH to facilitate SCP transfers. Depending on the device and its operating system, enabling SSH typically involves generating SSH key pairs for secure authentication, setting up SSH server settings, and ensuring that the device is configured to accept secure connections.

Once SSH is enabled, the next step is configuring the network devices for SCP file transfers. SCP requires both the client and the server to be set up to allow secure file transfers. On the client device, administrators will need to specify the destination device's IP address or hostname, along with the path where the files should be transferred. The device that will receive the files, or the server, also needs to have SCP configured to accept incoming connections. This involves ensuring that the server's SSH configuration allows for SCP file transfer and that appropriate file permissions are set on the directories where files are to be copied to or from.

One critical aspect of configuring SCP on devices is managing user authentication. SCP uses SSH key-based authentication to secure file transfers, which is more reliable and secure than using passwords. This authentication process involves generating a public and private key pair. The private key is kept securely on the client device, while the public key is installed on the server device. When a file transfer is initiated, the client sends a request to the server, and the server verifies the authenticity of the client by checking the public key against the list of authorized keys stored on the server. If the key matches, the server grants access, allowing the file transfer to proceed. This form of authentication ensures that only authorized users or devices can initiate file transfers, protecting sensitive information from unauthorized access.

After setting up SSH and ensuring proper authentication, administrators can configure file transfer commands using SCP. SCP commands are typically issued through a command-line interface, where administrators specify the source and destination paths for the file transfer. For example, a common SCP command to copy a configuration file from a local device to a remote server might look like this: scp /path/to/local/config.txt user@remote_host:/path/to/remote/destination. This command tells the client device to copy the specified configuration file to the specified location on the remote device. If transferring files in the other direction, the syntax is adjusted accordingly, allowing administrators to retrieve files from the server. The simplicity of the SCP command makes it easy to perform basic file transfer tasks, but it is also flexible enough for more complex configurations and automated scripts.

In addition to basic file transfers, SCP can be used for batch processing and automating file transfers. Network administrators often need to back up multiple configuration files or update software on several devices at once. SCP supports automation by allowing administrators to write scripts that schedule file transfers or automate tasks. For example, a script can be set up to back up configuration files from a range of network devices to a central server at regular intervals. This eliminates the need for manual intervention, saving time and reducing the risk of human error. Automation ensures that configuration files are always up-to-date and readily available for recovery in case of device failure or misconfiguration.

A crucial consideration when configuring SCP on devices is ensuring that the network environment is secure. Although SCP encrypts file transfers, administrators must still take steps to protect the devices involved. One essential measure is to configure firewalls and access control lists (ACLs) to restrict access to the SCP service. By limiting SCP access to specific IP addresses or subnets, administrators can prevent unauthorized devices from initiating file transfers. In addition to network access controls, administrators should also enforce strong password policies for user accounts, implement regular key rotation, and monitor SCP activity through logging to detect any potential security breaches or unauthorized access attempts.

Another important consideration when configuring SCP for secure file transfers is ensuring that the file transfer process is reliable and error-free. SCP provides some basic mechanisms for error checking, such as the use of hash functions to verify file integrity, but it does not have advanced error recovery features. If a file transfer is interrupted or corrupted during transmission, administrators must manually verify the transfer and, if necessary, restart the process. In networks where large files or frequent transfers are involved, administrators may need to consider other protocols, such as SFTP, that offer more robust error handling and the ability to resume interrupted transfers.

When configuring SCP on network devices, it is also essential to understand the limitations of the protocol. While SCP is highly secure and efficient, it is primarily focused on file transfer and lacks more advanced features, such as file manipulation capabilities. For example, SCP does not support directory listing, file renaming, or deleting files remotely. This makes SCP less suitable for situations where more comprehensive file management is required. In these cases, administrators might opt to use other protocols like SFTP, which offers more comprehensive file management features while still providing secure file transfers.

Additionally, SCP relies heavily on SSH for encryption and authentication, which means that the SSH service must be properly configured and maintained. Network administrators must ensure that SSH is always up to date and configured securely to prevent vulnerabilities from being exploited. This includes regularly patching SSH-related software, using strong encryption algorithms, and disabling unnecessary features that might expose the system to risks.

As network environments continue to grow in complexity, configuring SCP on devices becomes even more critical for maintaining secure and efficient file transfers. The ability to transfer configuration files, software updates, and other sensitive data securely across networks ensures that network devices remain properly configured and protected from potential threats. By following best practices for SCP configuration, including SSH setup, authentication management, file transfer automation, and network security, administrators can maintain the integrity and confidentiality of their network systems and reduce the risks associated with insecure file transfers. This makes SCP an essential tool in the broader toolkit of network administrators tasked with securing and managing network configurations.

SCP vs. TFTP: A Comparative Analysis

When it comes to transferring files across networks, two commonly used protocols are the Secure Copy Protocol (SCP) and the Trivial File Transfer Protocol (TFTP). Both protocols serve the same basic function of transferring files between systems, but they differ significantly in terms of security, functionality, and typical use cases. Understanding these differences is crucial for network administrators, as the choice between SCP and TFTP can have important implications for network security, efficiency, and ease of management.

The most significant difference between SCP and TFTP lies in their security features. SCP was designed with security in mind, built on the foundations of the Secure Shell (SSH) protocol. This provides strong encryption for both the control and data channels, ensuring that files transferred via SCP are protected against interception and tampering. SCP also employs SSH key-based authentication, which adds another layer of security by ensuring that only authorized users can initiate file transfers. In contrast, TFTP is a much simpler protocol that operates over the User Datagram Protocol (UDP) and does not offer any encryption or authentication. All data transferred using TFTP, including usernames, passwords, and file contents, is sent in plain text. This makes TFTP highly vulnerable to man-in-the-middle attacks, eavesdropping, and unauthorized access, especially on untrusted networks.

Because of its lack of encryption and authentication, TFTP is generally considered unsuitable for transferring sensitive or critical data. It is typically used in controlled environments, such as within isolated networks or when transferring non-sensitive files. For example, TFTP is commonly used in network boot scenarios, where devices need to retrieve boot images or configuration files from a central server in a trusted environment. On the other hand, SCP is well-suited for environments where security is paramount. It is widely used to transfer sensitive configuration files, backup data, and software updates, as it ensures the confidentiality and integrity of the transferred information.

Another key distinction between SCP and TFTP is the level of functionality they provide. TFTP is a minimalistic protocol, designed for simplicity and speed. It allows files to be transferred from one system to another, but it lacks many of the features that more advanced file transfer protocols offer. TFTP does not support file manipulation features such as listing directories, renaming files, or modifying file permissions. Its primary function is to transfer files between devices, and it excels in environments where simple, fast transfers are needed. However, this simplicity comes at a cost. TFTP lacks error recovery mechanisms, meaning that if a transfer is interrupted or corrupted, the client and server will not automatically retry or recover the file. This limitation can be problematic in environments where data integrity is critical.

SCP, by contrast, is a more robust protocol that offers additional functionality, such as error checking and verification of file integrity. SCP performs a hash check of the transferred file to ensure that it is not corrupted during the transfer process. If the file is incomplete or altered, SCP will not complete the transfer, preventing corrupted files from being delivered to the destination system. SCP also supports more advanced file management tasks, such as file permissions and ownership, which makes it suitable for more complex operations. Administrators can use SCP to securely transfer not only files but also entire directories, while also preserving the file system's structure and attributes. This makes SCP a more versatile option for file transfers in environments where the need for error recovery and comprehensive file management is more critical.

The performance of both SCP and TFTP is another important consideration. TFTP's simplicity and reliance on UDP contribute to its speed and low overhead. Because TFTP does not establish a connection before transferring data, it is faster than many other protocols, especially in environments where the network is stable and the file size is small. However, TFTP's reliance on UDP also means that it lacks the reliability of more robust protocols. UDP does not guarantee packet delivery, which can lead to dropped or corrupted packets in unstable networks. TFTP also does not have built-in mechanisms to resume interrupted transfers, which can be problematic when dealing with large files or unreliable networks.

SCP, on the other hand, uses SSH, which operates over TCP. TCP is a connection-oriented protocol that guarantees reliable packet delivery, meaning that SCP transfers are more resilient to network instability. However, the overhead introduced by TCP and SSH encryption can make SCP slower than TFTP in certain scenarios, particularly when transferring small files over stable networks. Despite this, the added reliability, error-checking features, and encryption make SCP a better choice for environments where security and file integrity are more important than raw speed. SCP's ability to resume interrupted transfers is another advantage, particularly when working with larger files or networks that experience occasional instability.

In terms of network configuration and ease of use, TFTP is generally easier to configure than SCP. TFTP servers are lightweight and simple to set up, with minimal configuration required. Most devices that support TFTP can be easily configured to send or receive files with just a few commands. This makes TFTP an appealing choice for network administrators looking for a quick and straightforward solution for file transfers in smaller, less security-conscious environments. On the other hand, SCP requires SSH to be configured on both the client and the server, which may involve additional setup and key management. SSH key-based authentication adds a layer of complexity, particularly in large environments where managing keys can become cumbersome. Additionally, because SCP is typically used in more secure environments, administrators need to ensure that firewalls and access control lists (ACLs) are properly configured to allow SCP traffic.

TFTP's primary use case is in network booting or simple file transfers in isolated, trusted environments. It is commonly employed to load boot images onto devices or retrieve configuration files for network devices like routers and switches. In contrast, SCP is typically used in more diverse and secure environments, where sensitive files need to be transferred between servers, workstations, or network devices. SCP's security features make it the protocol of choice for transferring configuration backups, software updates, and other critical files that require protection from unauthorized access or tampering.

The decision to use SCP or TFTP depends on the specific needs of the network environment. If speed and simplicity are the most important factors, and the files being transferred are not sensitive, TFTP can be an excellent choice. However, for secure file transfers that require encryption, authentication, and error recovery, SCP is the clear winner. SCP's robust security features, combined with its ability to verify file integrity and handle larger, more complex transfers, make it the preferred option for network administrators managing sensitive data or large-scale deployments. By understanding the key differences between SCP and TFTP, administrators can make informed decisions about which protocol best meets the needs of their network environment.

Troubleshooting SCP File Transfers

When it comes to securely transferring files across a network, the Secure Copy Protocol (SCP) is a popular choice due to its integration with the Secure Shell (SSH) protocol, which provides encryption and authentication. However, like any protocol, SCP is not immune to issues that can prevent successful file transfers. Network administrators who rely on SCP to move critical files must be prepared to troubleshoot common problems that may arise during transfers. These issues can stem from various factors, including network configurations, authentication failures, or software problems. A structured approach to troubleshooting SCP file transfers is essential for ensuring that files are transferred securely and efficiently.

The first step in troubleshooting SCP file transfers is verifying the network connectivity between the client and the server. SCP relies on SSH for communication, which means that both systems must be able to establish a network connection to each other. If there are issues with network connectivity, the SCP transfer will fail to initiate or complete. One of the most basic tests is to ping the remote server from the client system. A failed ping indicates that there is a network issue, such as an incorrect IP address or a firewall blocking traffic. If the server is unreachable, network administrators should verify the network settings on both the client and server, including checking routing tables, DNS configurations, and ensuring there are no issues with intermediate devices, such as routers or switches.

In addition to basic network connectivity, firewall settings play a crucial role in ensuring that SCP transfers can occur smoothly. SCP operates over SSH, which typically uses TCP port 22 by default. If either the client or server is behind a firewall, it is necessary to ensure that TCP port 22 is open for inbound and outbound traffic. Firewalls that block port 22 will prevent SCP from establishing a connection, resulting in transfer failures. Administrators should check the firewall rules on both the client and server systems, as well as any network firewalls, to ensure that SCP traffic is allowed. This is especially important in corporate or cloud environments where strict security measures often restrict network traffic. If SCP is blocked by a firewall, configuring the firewall to allow TCP port 22 or other designated ports for SSH traffic should resolve the issue.

Another common issue that may occur during SCP file transfers is authentication failure. SCP uses SSH for both encryption and authentication, meaning that proper credentials must be provided to initiate a transfer. Authentication failures are often caused by issues with SSH key pairs, which are used to securely authenticate the client and the server. In SSH-based authentication, the client generates a private key and shares the corresponding public key with the server. If the keys are not correctly configured or mismatched, SCP will fail to authenticate the client. Administrators should first check that the correct SSH key pair is being used and that the public key is properly installed in the authorized_keys file on the server. It is also important to verify that the permissions on the key files are correct, as improperly configured permissions can prevent successful authentication. For example, the authorized_keys file on the server must have strict permissions, such as 600, to ensure that it is only readable by the root user.

Another factor to consider when troubleshooting SCP authentication is the use of password-based authentication. Although SSH key-based authentication is recommended for better security, some systems may be configured to accept password authentication instead. If the server is set up to use password-based authentication, administrators should verify that the correct username and password are being used. Additionally, the SSH configuration on the server may have restrictions that prevent password authentication or require additional configuration steps. It is essential to check the SSH server's configuration file (typically located at /etc/ssh/sshd_config) and ensure that the settings for password authentication are correctly defined.

If the authentication process is successful but the file transfer still fails, the issue may be related to file permissions on either the client or the server. SCP requires that the user has the necessary read permissions on the source file and write permissions on the destination directory. If the file being transferred is inaccessible due to permissions restrictions, SCP will be unable to complete the transfer. Administrators should verify that the file permissions on the source file are set to allow the client user to read the file. Likewise, the destination directory on the server must have write permissions for the user or group performing the transfer. If the permissions are incorrect, they must be adjusted to allow the SCP process to complete successfully.

SCP also has limitations when it comes to handling large files or unstable network conditions. SCP does not support features like automatic file resume or error recovery, which can be problematic when transferring large files or when network connections are unreliable. If a file transfer is interrupted or times out, SCP will not automatically resume the transfer, requiring the entire file to be transferred again. This can result in significant delays, especially when working with large datasets. In these cases, administrators may need to ensure that the network connection is stable or consider using alternative protocols, such as SFTP, which offer features like file transfer resumption and better error handling. Additionally, administrators can try to increase the SSH timeout settings to prevent premature disconnections during longer file transfers.

Another potential issue is the SSH service itself. SCP relies on SSH to secure communication between the client and the server. If the SSH service is not running or has encountered an error, SCP transfers will fail to establish a connection. Administrators should ensure that the SSH service is up and running on both the client and server systems.

They can check the status of the SSH service using system commands such as "systemctl status sshd" on Linux-based systems or by verifying the SSH service status in the system logs. Restarting the SSH service may resolve any transient issues that are preventing SCP from functioning correctly.

In some cases, SCP file transfers may fail due to the use of incompatible SSH versions or configurations. Newer versions of SSH may introduce changes that are not compatible with older versions, resulting in failed connections or transfers. Administrators should ensure that both the client and server are running compatible versions of SSH and that their configurations align. If necessary, updating or downgrading the SSH version on either the client or the server can resolve compatibility issues.

Lastly, if SCP commands are not being executed correctly, it is important to check for syntax errors or other issues with the command itself. SCP commands must include the correct syntax, specifying the source file and destination path, and must also include the appropriate authentication parameters. Administrators should review the command line for any errors, such as missing file paths or incorrect user credentials, that could be causing the transfer to fail.

Troubleshooting SCP file transfers requires a methodical approach to address issues related to network connectivity, authentication, file permissions, and service configurations. By carefully checking the configuration of both the client and the server, ensuring that the network environment is properly set up, and addressing potential issues with SSH keys and file permissions, administrators can quickly resolve most SCP-related problems. Additionally, understanding the limitations of SCP, such as its inability to resume interrupted transfers, will help administrators choose the appropriate protocol for different use cases. By following these troubleshooting steps, network administrators can ensure that SCP operates smoothly and securely for file transfers across their network.

Advanced SCP Usage: Automation and Scripting

The Secure Copy Protocol (SCP) is widely used for securely transferring files across networks, leveraging the encryption and authentication features of the Secure Shell (SSH) protocol. SCP's simplicity and reliability make it a powerful tool for network administrators, but its true potential is realized when it is combined with automation and scripting. Automation in SCP allows administrators to streamline file transfer tasks, minimize human intervention, and ensure consistency in network management. By using scripts, administrators can schedule, automate, and manage SCP file transfers more effectively, enhancing both efficiency and security in network operations.

One of the most powerful aspects of SCP is its ability to be automated through scripting, enabling administrators to configure and initiate file transfers without having to manually execute commands each time. Automation can be achieved through various scripting languages such as Bash, Python, or Perl. These scripts can be used to create custom workflows for transferring files, managing backups, or synchronizing configurations across multiple devices. For example, an administrator can create a script to regularly back up configuration files from network devices to a centralized server, ensuring that the most recent versions of the configurations are always available for recovery.

The process of automating SCP file transfers begins with setting up a basic SCP command within a script. The SCP command requires at least two arguments: the source file and the destination path. By embedding this command in a script, administrators can dynamically specify the files to be transferred, the source and destination paths, and the credentials for authentication. For example, a basic Bash script for transferring a file from a local machine to a remote server might look like this:

```
scp /path/to/local/file
user@remote_host:/path/to/remote/destination
```

This simple script can be extended to automate more complex tasks, such as transferring multiple files, backing up directories, or managing file permissions. One of the key benefits of using SCP in automation is the ability to schedule these file transfers to occur at regular intervals, such as nightly backups or periodic configuration updates. This ensures that critical files are consistently transferred without the need for constant manual oversight.

Scheduling SCP file transfers is often achieved by integrating scripts with system scheduling tools. On Unix-like systems, tools such as cron allow administrators to schedule tasks at specified intervals. A cron job can be configured to execute the SCP script at a specific time, such as every night at midnight, ensuring that the backup or file transfer occurs automatically. For example, to schedule a script that backs up configuration files every day at 2 a.m., an entry in the crontab file might look like this:

```
0 2 * * * /path/to/scp-backup-script.sh
```

This allows the administrator to automate regular tasks without needing to manually trigger the transfers, providing peace of mind that the tasks will be performed consistently and on time. Automating SCP file transfers through cron jobs is especially useful for network administrators who manage multiple devices and need to ensure that critical files are regularly backed up or synchronized.

Advanced SCP usage can also include automating file transfers to multiple destinations simultaneously. In environments where multiple network devices require the same configuration files, SCP can be used to distribute the files to multiple servers or devices with a single command. This is particularly useful for updating configurations or software on several devices at once. A script can be written to loop through a list of devices and execute the SCP command for each device, transferring the required files to each destination in a batch process. This reduces the need for repetitive manual tasks and ensures that all devices are updated consistently.

Another powerful feature of SCP in automation is its integration with version control systems. For example, SCP can be used to push updates from a local version-controlled directory to remote devices. By integrating SCP with Git or another version control system, administrators can automate the process of deploying the latest configuration files or software updates to devices based on the most recent commit or change. This helps maintain consistency across devices and ensures that the most up-to-date files are always in place, reducing the likelihood of configuration drift and improving overall network reliability.

When working with SCP in automation, it is essential to manage SSH keys effectively, especially in environments where scripts are running without manual intervention. Using SSH key-based authentication is critical for automating SCP transfers securely, as it eliminates the need to enter passwords each time a file transfer occurs. Administrators must ensure that the appropriate SSH keys are generated, stored securely, and authorized on both the client and server systems. By using SSH keys, scripts can securely initiate SCP file transfers without compromising security, as long as the private keys are kept secure and protected with strong passphrases.

However, administrators should be aware of the need to manage and rotate SSH keys periodically to maintain a high level of security. Storing private keys in secure locations and limiting access to them is essential for preventing unauthorized access to network devices. Additionally, using passphrase protection for private keys provides an added layer of security, ensuring that even if the private key is compromised, the attacker cannot use it without the passphrase.

Another consideration when automating SCP file transfers is the handling of errors and logging. While SCP is a robust and reliable protocol, issues such as network interruptions or authentication failures can occur during file transfers. It is essential to include error-handling mechanisms in SCP scripts to detect and respond to these issues. Administrators can implement checks to verify whether the file transfer was successful, such as checking the return status of the SCP command. If an error occurs, the script can be designed to retry the transfer, log the error, or send notifications to the administrator. For example, a Bash script might include an error check like this:

```
scp /path/to/local/file
user@remote_host:/path/to/remote/destination || echo "SCP transfer
failed" >> /path/to/logfile.log
```

This ensures that errors are logged and can be reviewed later, helping administrators identify and resolve issues that might have affected the file transfer process.

Furthermore, administrators can integrate SCP file transfers with network monitoring tools to gain insights into transfer performance. By monitoring the time it takes to complete transfers and the amount of data being moved, administrators can identify bottlenecks or inefficiencies in the transfer process. Integrating SCP with performance monitoring tools allows for proactive management of file transfer operations and helps ensure that automated tasks do not interfere with the overall network performance.

Scripting and automation in SCP provide network administrators with a powerful toolkit for managing file transfers in a secure, efficient, and scalable manner. Whether automating routine backups, updating configurations across multiple devices, or integrating SCP with version control systems, the ability to script and schedule SCP transfers enables administrators to reduce manual effort, minimize errors, and ensure that critical files are consistently and securely transferred. The combination of SCP's security features and automation capabilities makes it an invaluable tool for network management, streamlining tasks and enhancing the overall efficiency of the network infrastructure.

The Role of SFTP in Configuration Management

In modern network management, the secure transfer of configuration files, software updates, and other sensitive data is paramount to ensuring the integrity and security of a network. The Secure File Transfer Protocol (SFTP) plays a significant role in configuration management by providing a secure, encrypted method for transferring files between systems. Unlike older, insecure protocols such as TFTP, SFTP uses the Secure Shell (SSH) protocol for encryption, making it an essential tool for managing configurations and ensuring the protection of critical files during transfer. SFTP is widely used by network administrators to maintain consistency across devices, automate processes, and safeguard the integrity of sensitive configuration data.

SFTP was designed as an improvement over traditional FTP, which lacked encryption and authentication features. FTP transfers data in plaintext, making it vulnerable to eavesdropping and attacks, particularly on untrusted networks. In contrast, SFTP encrypts both the control and data channels, ensuring that all files transferred between systems remain confidential and protected from tampering. This security feature is especially important in configuration management, where configuration files often contain sensitive information, such as system settings, user credentials, and access control policies. By using SFTP, administrators can ensure that these critical files are securely transferred without exposing them to potential threats.

One of the key advantages of SFTP in configuration management is its ability to support secure authentication. SFTP uses SSH for both encryption and authentication, which is typically done using SSH key pairs. This authentication method is far more secure than traditional password-based authentication, as it involves cryptographic keys instead of easily guessable passwords. The use of SSH key pairs ensures that only authorized users can access the configuration files, preventing unauthorized devices from gaining access to critical network data. For example, administrators can configure SFTP to only allow file transfers from trusted systems that have the appropriate SSH private keys. This adds a layer of access control and ensures that only those with proper credentials can make changes to configuration files or retrieve sensitive information.

Another important feature of SFTP is its ability to provide a complete file management system. Unlike TFTP or SCP, which are primarily used for simple file transfers, SFTP offers a full range of file manipulation features. Administrators can not only upload and download configuration files but also rename files, delete files, and navigate directories on the remote server. This flexibility is crucial in configuration management, as it allows administrators to perform a variety of file management tasks without needing to rely on separate tools or protocols. For example, administrators can use SFTP to download a configuration file, edit it locally, and then upload the modified file to the server, all while maintaining the security of the transfer.

SFTP also includes features for verifying the integrity of transferred files. When transferring configuration files, it is essential to ensure that the file has not been altered or corrupted during the transfer process. SFTP includes built-in mechanisms for verifying file integrity, such as checksums or hash verification, which ensure that the file on the receiving system matches the file that was sent. This is especially important in configuration management, where even small errors or changes to configuration files can lead to network instability, security vulnerabilities, or system failures. By using SFTP, administrators can be confident that the transferred files are accurate and intact, reducing the risk of issues arising from corrupted or incomplete file transfers.

Automation is another area where SFTP plays a vital role in configuration management. Network administrators often need to perform routine tasks such as backing up configurations, updating firmware, or synchronizing configurations across multiple devices. Automating these tasks with SFTP helps streamline the process and ensures that these critical operations are performed regularly without manual intervention. For example, administrators can write scripts that use SFTP to automatically back up configuration files from network devices to a central server on a scheduled basis. This ensures that the most up-to-date configuration files are always available for recovery in case of a failure, without requiring manual backups each time. Automation not only saves time but also reduces the risk of human error, ensuring consistency and reliability across the network.

In large, distributed networks, where multiple devices need to be regularly updated or reconfigured, SFTP provides a scalable solution for configuration management. By using SFTP to transfer configuration files between servers, routers, switches, and firewalls, administrators can maintain consistency across the entire network. For example, in an organization with several branch offices, administrators can use SFTP to push configuration updates to all remote devices simultaneously, ensuring that all devices are running the same configuration and that any security patches or policy changes are applied consistently. This level of control and consistency is essential for managing complex network infrastructures and maintaining network security.

SFTP also plays a significant role in compliance and auditing, especially in industries that require strict regulatory adherence, such as finance, healthcare, and government. Many of these industries mandate that sensitive data, including configuration files, must be transferred and stored securely. By using SFTP, organizations can ensure that their file transfer practices meet these compliance requirements. SFTP provides encrypted data transfers and secure authentication, both of which are necessary for meeting regulatory standards. Additionally, because SFTP supports detailed logging of file transfer activities, administrators can maintain an audit trail that records when files were transferred, who initiated the transfer, and whether the transfer was successful. This auditability is crucial for organizations that need to demonstrate compliance with industry regulations or internal security policies.

Despite its many advantages, there are some limitations to using SFTP in configuration management. One of the primary drawbacks is that SFTP requires a more complex setup compared to simpler protocols like TFTP or SCP. Administrators must configure SSH on both the client and server, manage SSH key pairs, and ensure that proper access controls are in place. This setup process can be time-consuming, particularly in large environments with many devices. Additionally, while SFTP provides strong encryption and security, the overhead of encrypting and decrypting data can introduce some performance degradation, especially when transferring large files over slow or congested networks.

Moreover, SFTP is typically more resource-intensive than other file transfer protocols, as it requires running the SSH service on both the client and server systems. This additional resource usage may be a concern in environments with limited processing power or bandwidth. However, for most modern networks, the benefits of secure file transfers far outweigh the performance trade-offs, particularly when dealing with sensitive configuration files or compliance-driven requirements.

SFTP's role in configuration management is indispensable for network administrators who need to ensure the secure, reliable, and efficient transfer of configuration files. With its strong encryption, comprehensive file management capabilities, automation features, and support for error checking and integrity verification, SFTP is the ideal protocol for transferring sensitive configuration data. As network environments become more complex and security becomes a higher priority, the role of SFTP in configuration management will continue to grow, helping administrators manage their networks more securely and efficiently. By integrating SFTP into their workflow, organizations can maintain secure, consistent, and compliant configuration management practices across their entire network infrastructure.

FTP vs. SCP: Differences and Use Cases

When it comes to transferring files across a network, administrators are often faced with choosing between various protocols that serve different needs and use cases. Among the most widely used protocols are the File Transfer Protocol (FTP) and the Secure Copy Protocol (SCP). Both protocols facilitate the movement of files between systems, but they have distinct characteristics that make them more suitable for specific scenarios. Understanding the differences between FTP and SCP is essential for making the right decision regarding their use, especially in network environments where security, speed, and functionality are key concerns.

The most notable difference between FTP and SCP lies in their security features. FTP, in its traditional form, does not provide encryption for the data being transferred. This lack of security means that any data, including sensitive files and login credentials, is transmitted in clear text, making it vulnerable to interception and unauthorized access. In contrast, SCP leverages the Secure Shell (SSH) protocol to encrypt both the control and data channels during the file transfer process. This encryption ensures that all files transferred using SCP are protected against eavesdropping, man-in-the-middle attacks, and tampering. The inherent security provided by SCP makes it the preferred choice for environments where data confidentiality and integrity are paramount.

FTP, however, does offer some degree of security when used in conjunction with the FTPS extension, which adds encryption via SSL/TLS. While FTPS addresses many of the security concerns inherent in traditional FTP, it still operates with a less secure design than SCP.

FTP, even with FTPS, requires multiple ports to be open, which can complicate network configurations, particularly in environments with strict firewall rules. Additionally, while FTPS secures the control channel for authentication, the data channel may still be vulnerable to attacks if not properly configured. SCP, on the other hand, operates over a single secure channel using SSH, simplifying firewall configurations and minimizing potential security risks.

Another key difference between FTP and SCP lies in the level of functionality they provide. FTP is a more feature-rich protocol compared to SCP. FTP supports a variety of commands that enable file manipulation on the remote server, such as renaming files, listing directories, and deleting files. These features make FTP a versatile option for users who need to perform comprehensive file management tasks in addition to simple file transfers. In contrast, SCP is designed to be a simple, no-frills protocol that focuses on transferring files securely between systems. SCP does not support advanced file manipulation features. It is primarily concerned with copying files from one system to another, and its operations are limited to file transfers only.

SCP's simplicity, however, is an advantage in environments where security is the top priority, and the need for additional file management capabilities is minimal. SCP's straightforward nature allows for quick and easy configuration and operation, making it an ideal choice when security and speed are more important than complex file management tasks. For example, in a network where administrators need to securely back up configuration files or transfer firmware updates to remote devices, SCP is a better choice due to its secure, efficient design.

Performance is another factor to consider when comparing FTP and SCP. FTP tends to be faster than SCP in some cases, particularly when dealing with large files or high-volume file transfers. This is partly because FTP operates over the Transmission Control Protocol (TCP), which establishes a reliable connection and guarantees the delivery of data. TCP's error-checking mechanisms ensure that files are delivered intact, and FTP's multi-threading capabilities can accelerate the transfer of large files. However, FTP's performance advantage may diminish in environments where security is required, as the protocol's lack of encryption and reliance on multiple open ports can lead to increased overhead in more complex network setups.

On the other hand, SCP, while slower than FTP in some cases, is optimized for secure file transfers and tends to perform better in environments where security is more important than raw speed. SCP uses SSH for both encryption and authentication, which adds overhead to the process and can slow down transfers. However, SCP's performance is more than sufficient for transferring smaller files or in environments where sensitive information is being exchanged, as the encryption ensures the integrity and confidentiality of the files being transferred. For scenarios that demand a balance between security and performance, SCP may be preferred despite its slightly lower transfer speeds compared to FTP.

Both FTP and SCP have distinct use cases, and understanding these scenarios can help administrators choose the appropriate protocol based on their specific needs. FTP remains popular for general-purpose file transfers, particularly in environments where security is not a primary concern. It is well-suited for transferring large volumes of data in internal networks or trusted environments where the risk of interception is low. FTP is also a good choice when advanced file management features, such as directory listing and file manipulation, are required. For instance, in scenarios where users need to upload and download files to and from a remote server while managing directories, FTP provides the necessary functionality.

In contrast, SCP is more suitable for situations where secure file transfers are essential. For network administrators responsible for managing the configuration files of network devices or transferring sensitive data, SCP offers a much more secure solution. SCP is commonly used for transferring configuration files between systems or backing up critical data, especially in scenarios where the data must be kept confidential and protected from tampering. Additionally, SCP is often used in automated processes, such as scripting and scheduled backups, to ensure that sensitive files are securely transferred at regular intervals.

SCP is also ideal for remote file transfers in highly secure environments, such as government or military networks, where strict security requirements must be met. It is also widely used by developers and system administrators who need to securely transfer source code, binaries, or software updates between servers or between local machines and remote systems. In these cases, SCP's secure nature ensures that the files are protected during the transfer process, reducing the likelihood of data breaches or security incidents.

In environments where speed is of the essence and security is less of a concern, FTP may still be a suitable option. For example, in internal networks where large volumes of data need to be transferred quickly between trusted systems, FTP's speed and ease of use make it an efficient solution. Furthermore, FTP is commonly used in scenarios where file transfers are not the only task at hand, such as when managing websites or providing access to large sets of files for download. In such cases, FTP's versatility and speed outweigh its security limitations.

The decision between FTP and SCP ultimately depends on the specific requirements of the environment. When security is paramount, such as when transferring sensitive configurations or critical system files, SCP is the obvious choice. On the other hand, if the priority is speed and the network environment is trusted, FTP may be the better option. Understanding the strengths and weaknesses of each protocol allows network administrators to select the most appropriate tool for each situation, ensuring that file transfers are both efficient and secure.

Integrating SCP and TFTP into a Network Management Strategy

In modern network environments, ensuring the efficient management and transfer of configuration files, firmware, and other essential data is vital for maintaining system integrity and reducing downtime. Two protocols that play a critical role in this process are the Secure Copy Protocol (SCP) and the Trivial File Transfer Protocol (TFTP). Both protocols are widely used for transferring files across networks, but they serve different purposes and offer distinct advantages and disadvantages. Integrating SCP and TFTP into a network management strategy involves understanding their respective use cases and determining how to leverage both protocols effectively to optimize network performance, security, and reliability.

SCP is primarily used for secure file transfers. It utilizes the Secure Shell (SSH) protocol for encryption, which ensures that data, including sensitive configuration files and backup data, is protected during transfer. The use of SSH not only encrypts the data but also provides authentication, ensuring that only authorized users can access the files being transferred. This makes SCP an essential tool in environments where security is paramount. Whether administrators are transferring configuration files between devices or performing system backups, SCP ensures that all data is transmitted securely, preventing unauthorized access or data tampering. It is particularly useful when transferring sensitive or critical data that must remain confidential, such as system credentials, access control lists, and network configurations.

On the other hand, TFTP is a simpler, less secure protocol that operates over UDP and is commonly used in situations where speed and efficiency are more important than security. TFTP is often used for tasks such as network booting, where devices need to retrieve boot images or firmware updates from a centralized server. In environments where network devices, such as routers, switches, and firewalls, need to be quickly and efficiently updated with configuration files or software images, TFTP provides a lightweight solution that minimizes overhead and facilitates rapid file transfers. However, TFTP's lack of encryption and authentication makes it unsuitable for transferring sensitive data in environments where security is a concern.

The key to integrating SCP and TFTP into a cohesive network management strategy is to recognize the strengths and limitations of each protocol and apply them where they are most appropriate. SCP's strong security features make it ideal for transferring sensitive files, while TFTP's simplicity and speed make it well-suited for tasks that do not involve critical or confidential data. A well-rounded network management strategy will often require the use of both protocols to meet the varying needs of different tasks within the network.

One common use case for SCP in a network management strategy is the secure transfer of configuration files and system backups. Network administrators often rely on regular backups of configuration files to ensure that they can quickly restore devices in the event of a failure or misconfiguration. SCP allows administrators to securely back up configuration files from routers, switches, firewalls, and servers to a central backup server. By scheduling these backups to occur automatically at regular intervals, administrators can ensure that they always have access to the most up-to-date configurations in case of an emergency. Furthermore, because SCP encrypts both the data and the authentication process, administrators can rest assured that the files are protected from unauthorized access during transmission.

TFTP, on the other hand, is commonly used in scenarios where devices need to quickly retrieve firmware images or configuration files during boot-up. For example, network devices that are powered on or reset may use TFTP to load the necessary boot images or configurations. This is especially useful in environments where devices are frequently updated or replaced, as it allows for a centralized method of delivering the required files to multiple devices without the need for manual intervention. TFTP's speed and efficiency make it a perfect fit for these scenarios, where large numbers of devices need to quickly and automatically load their configurations or operating systems.

In many cases, network administrators can integrate both SCP and TFTP into a unified workflow to enhance the management of network devices. For instance, administrators can use TFTP to load the necessary configuration files or firmware updates onto devices during boot-up, while also using SCP to back up those configuration files securely to a central server. This approach ensures that devices are always up to date with the latest firmware and configurations, while also providing a secure and reliable method for backing up critical system data. By combining the strengths of both protocols, administrators can achieve a more efficient and secure network management process.

Automation plays a key role in optimizing the use of both SCP and TFTP in a network management strategy. Many network management tasks, such as backing up configurations or updating firmware, can be automated to reduce the need for manual intervention. By using scripting languages such as Bash or Python, administrators can automate the process of transferring files using SCP and TFTP, allowing for scheduled backups and updates to occur automatically at set intervals. For example, administrators can create scripts that automatically use SCP to back up configuration files from network devices every night, ensuring that the most recent configurations are always available for recovery in case of a failure. Similarly, administrators can automate the process of loading firmware updates onto devices using TFTP, reducing the time and effort required to perform these updates manually.

Integrating SCP and TFTP into a network management strategy also requires careful consideration of network security. While SCP provides strong encryption and authentication, TFTP's lack of security features makes it vulnerable to attacks such as eavesdropping and data tampering. As such, TFTP should only be used in trusted, isolated networks where security is not a primary concern. For example, TFTP can be used in a local network environment to quickly deploy firmware updates to devices that are behind a firewall or within a secure zone. However, when transferring sensitive data, such as configuration files or backups, administrators should always use SCP to ensure that the data remains encrypted and protected from unauthorized access.

Network administrators should also consider the scalability of their network management strategy when using SCP and TFTP. While both protocols are capable of transferring files across multiple devices, the volume of data and the number of devices in a network can impact the performance of file transfers. For example, TFTP may perform well in smaller networks with limited file sizes, but its lack of error checking and reliability may cause problems in larger, more complex networks. On the other hand, SCP's error-checking mechanisms and encryption features ensure that file transfers are secure and reliable, even in large-scale networks. Administrators should balance the use of both protocols to ensure that network management tasks are completed efficiently, without sacrificing security or performance.

By carefully integrating SCP and TFTP into their network management strategy, administrators can ensure that their network is both secure and efficient. SCP's security features make it an ideal choice for transferring sensitive configuration files and backups, while TFTP's simplicity and speed make it well-suited for tasks such as network booting and firmware updates. Through automation and thoughtful protocol selection, administrators can optimize their workflow and ensure that their network devices are always properly configured and up-to-date. Integrating both protocols allows for a flexible and secure approach to managing network devices, improving overall network reliability and performance.

The Role of Configuration Management Protocols in Automation

Configuration management is a critical aspect of modern network administration, ensuring that all devices and systems are properly configured and maintained. Automation has become a vital part of this process, allowing administrators to efficiently manage large and complex network infrastructures. Configuration management protocols, such as TFTP, SCP, SFTP, and others, play an essential role in automating the transfer and management of configuration files, firmware, and backups. By integrating these protocols into automation workflows, administrators can streamline their operations, minimize errors, and ensure consistency across the network.

One of the key functions of configuration management protocols in automation is enabling the secure and efficient transfer of configuration files between devices and central management systems. Network devices, such as routers, switches, firewalls, and servers, often require regular configuration updates, backups, and firmware upgrades. Manually performing these tasks on each device would be time-consuming, error-prone, and inefficient. By using protocols like SCP or SFTP in automation scripts, administrators can schedule regular configuration backups and updates, reducing the need for human intervention and ensuring that configurations are consistently applied across the network.

For example, administrators can automate the process of backing up the configuration files of network devices at regular intervals, ensuring that the most up-to-date versions of these files are always available. This process can be done without manual oversight, allowing the system to operate autonomously. Such automation ensures that if a device fails or a configuration needs to be restored, administrators can quickly recover the system using the most recent backup. The ability to automate these tasks with configuration management protocols significantly improves efficiency and reduces the risk of human error, which is a common cause of configuration issues.

The use of TFTP in network automation is particularly useful in scenarios where simplicity and speed are essential. TFTP's lightweight nature makes it an ideal protocol for transferring small configuration files or boot images to network devices during the boot-up process. Network devices often use TFTP to retrieve initial configurations or firmware images, enabling them to quickly become operational. By automating this process, administrators can ensure that new devices or devices that have been reset are automatically configured with the appropriate settings and images without manual intervention. This is particularly valuable in large-scale networks, where hundreds or even thousands of devices may need to be deployed or reconfigured at once. Automation reduces deployment time and ensures that each device receives the correct configuration, preventing inconsistencies that could lead to network issues.

SCP, on the other hand, is more suitable for secure file transfers and is often used in automation scenarios where encryption and authentication are critical. SCP uses SSH for both secure file transfer and authentication, ensuring that the configuration files and other sensitive data are protected during transmission. Automating the use of SCP for transferring configuration files helps to maintain security standards across the network. Administrators can use SCP to regularly push configuration updates or firmware patches to devices while ensuring that the data remains secure and protected from potential threats. By incorporating SCP into automation workflows, administrators can create a more secure network environment and streamline the management of sensitive data.

Another important role that configuration management protocols play in automation is ensuring consistency and compliance across the network. In large or complex networks, ensuring that all devices are configured according to the same standards and policies is essential for maintaining network stability and security. Automation tools that integrate configuration management protocols can be used to push standardized configuration files to all devices in the network. This helps to ensure that configurations are consistently applied and that devices comply with organizational policies, industry standards, and regulatory requirements. By automating this process, administrators can avoid the inconsistencies that might arise from manual configuration, reducing the risk of misconfigurations that could lead to security vulnerabilities or operational issues.

In addition to consistency, automation with configuration management protocols also enables faster response times in the event of changes or incidents. When a change is needed in the configuration of multiple devices, administrators can use automation scripts to rapidly deploy the updated configuration files across the entire network. This ensures that devices are updated quickly, reducing downtime and minimizing the disruption caused by manual updates. Similarly, in the event of a security incident or system failure, automated processes can quickly restore devices to their previous working configurations, ensuring continuity of service and faster recovery times.

Automation in configuration management also allows for easier scaling of network operations. As networks grow in size and complexity, managing configurations manually becomes increasingly difficult. Configuration management protocols such as SCP and TFTP, when integrated into automation systems, enable administrators to scale their operations more effectively. With automated file transfers and updates, administrators can manage thousands of devices with ease, ensuring that configuration changes are applied uniformly and that backups are regularly taken. The ability to scale these processes efficiently is essential for large enterprises or service providers who need to maintain a large number of devices without sacrificing performance, security, or consistency.

The integration of configuration management protocols into automated workflows also improves the overall monitoring and auditing of network configurations. By automating the transfer and backup of configuration files, administrators can track changes and maintain an up-to-date inventory of all configurations across the network. This can be especially valuable for auditing purposes, as it provides a detailed record of when configurations were changed, who made the changes, and what changes were applied. In regulated industries, where compliance with standards such as ISO, HIPAA, or PCI-DSS is required, having automated systems that track configuration changes can simplify the audit process and provide greater visibility into network operations.

While automation with configuration management protocols offers numerous benefits, it is also important to consider the potential challenges and limitations of such systems. One challenge is ensuring the security of the automation environment itself. While SCP and SFTP offer encryption and authentication for data transfers, administrators must also secure the automation scripts and systems that manage these processes. This includes safeguarding the private keys used for SSH authentication, securing automation servers, and ensuring that automation scripts are not exposed to unauthorized users. By implementing robust security practices for the entire automation infrastructure, administrators can mitigate risks and maintain a secure network environment.

Another challenge is ensuring that automation processes do not conflict with existing network configurations or create unintended consequences. For example, if a configuration file is pushed to a device without proper testing or validation, it could inadvertently disrupt network operations. To address this, administrators should incorporate testing and validation steps into their automation workflows, ensuring that configuration changes are thoroughly vetted before being applied to production systems. Additionally, periodic reviews of automation scripts and processes are necessary to ensure that they continue to meet the evolving needs of the network.

Incorporating configuration management protocols like SCP and TFTP into automated workflows can significantly improve network management by enhancing security, consistency, and scalability. Automation reduces the time and effort required for routine tasks, such as configuration backups, firmware updates, and device deployments, while ensuring that these tasks are performed consistently and securely. With the proper integration and security measures, administrators can build efficient and reliable automation systems that streamline network management and improve operational efficiency. By leveraging these protocols, network administrators can maintain a secure, consistent, and well-managed network environment that supports the ongoing needs of the organization.

Dynamic Host Configuration Protocol (DHCP) and Its Relationship with Configuration Management

The Dynamic Host Configuration Protocol (DHCP) is a network management protocol that plays a vital role in automating the assignment of IP addresses and other network configuration parameters to devices on a network. It simplifies the process of managing IP addresses, reduces the potential for errors in network configuration, and ensures that network devices can easily connect to the network without the need for manual configuration. The integration of DHCP with configuration management is crucial for maintaining an efficient, scalable, and secure network infrastructure. By automating the allocation of network settings and ensuring consistency across devices, DHCP contributes significantly to the overall configuration management strategy of an organization.

DHCP operates by allowing network devices, such as computers, printers, or smartphones, to obtain an IP address and other necessary configuration details from a central server without requiring manual intervention. When a device connects to a network, it sends a broadcast request to the DHCP server, asking for an IP address and other relevant configuration information, such as the default gateway, DNS servers, and subnet mask. The DHCP server then responds by assigning an available IP address from a predefined pool, along with the necessary configuration parameters. This process eliminates the need for administrators to manually assign IP addresses to each device, reducing the administrative overhead and the likelihood of configuration errors.

In terms of configuration management, DHCP simplifies and automates the management of IP addresses within a network. In traditional networks where static IP addressing is used, administrators must manually assign and track IP addresses for each device. This process can be time-consuming, especially in large networks, and is prone to human error. With DHCP, however, the entire process is automated, ensuring that each device on the network receives a unique, valid IP address without the risk of conflicts. Additionally, DHCP allows for the centralization of network configuration management, as the DHCP server holds the configuration information for all devices on the network, ensuring consistency and reducing the administrative burden.

DHCP's relationship with configuration management extends beyond the assignment of IP addresses. The protocol also plays a key role in ensuring that network devices are properly configured with the necessary network settings. For example, when a device requests an IP address from the DHCP server, it also receives critical configuration parameters, such as the subnet mask, DNS servers, and default gateway. These parameters are essential for ensuring that the device can communicate effectively within the network and access external resources. By automating the assignment of these configuration settings, DHCP helps prevent misconfigurations and ensures that all devices on the network are properly configured for seamless communication.

Another important aspect of DHCP in configuration management is its role in network scalability. As organizations grow and their network infrastructure becomes more complex, the number of devices that need to be configured and managed increases. Manually assigning IP addresses and other configuration settings to each device can quickly become unmanageable in large networks. DHCP provides a scalable solution by automating the assignment of network settings, making it easier to add new devices to the network without requiring manual configuration. This is especially important in dynamic environments, such as those that involve frequent device additions, removals, or changes. With DHCP, devices can be automatically configured as they join the network, ensuring that they are assigned the appropriate settings without administrative intervention.

In addition to scalability, DHCP contributes to network security and reliability by enforcing consistent configuration policies. For example, network administrators can configure the DHCP server to assign specific IP address ranges to different types of devices, such as printers, servers, or workstations. This segmentation of devices based on their roles helps ensure that network resources are appropriately allocated and that devices are kept within the appropriate subnet. DHCP also helps prevent IP address conflicts, which can occur when two devices are assigned the same IP address. This is particularly important in larger networks where static IP addressing would require constant monitoring to ensure that address conflicts do not arise.

DHCP also enables more efficient management of IP address allocation through features like lease durations and address reservation. When a device requests an IP address from the DHCP server, it is typically assigned a lease, which is a temporary assignment that expires after a set period. This lease system allows the DHCP server to efficiently manage a limited pool of IP addresses by reusing addresses that are no longer in use. Additionally, administrators can configure address reservations for specific devices, ensuring that those devices always receive the same IP address each time they connect to the network. This is particularly useful for network devices that require a static IP address, such as servers or printers, but without the need for manual configuration.

The relationship between DHCP and configuration management also extends to monitoring and troubleshooting. DHCP servers maintain logs of all assigned IP addresses, lease times, and configuration settings. These logs are valuable for network administrators when diagnosing network issues, tracking device connectivity, or auditing network activity. By reviewing the DHCP server logs, administrators can identify which devices have been assigned specific IP addresses, monitor the status of IP address leases, and troubleshoot network problems. For example, if a device is experiencing connectivity issues, administrators can check the DHCP logs to verify whether the device received the correct IP address and configuration parameters. This information is critical for resolving network issues efficiently and ensuring that devices are properly configured.

In larger networks, where DHCP servers are often used in conjunction with other network management tools, such as DNS and IPAM (IP Address Management) systems, the integration of these systems with

DHCP further enhances configuration management. IPAM systems allow administrators to manage IP address allocation across the network, track IP address usage, and integrate with DHCP to automate the assignment of addresses. When combined with DNS, DHCP ensures that devices not only receive an IP address but also have their hostnames automatically registered in the DNS system, enabling seamless communication across the network. This integration of DHCP with other network management tools provides a unified approach to managing network configurations and ensures that all devices are properly configured and accessible.

The role of DHCP in configuration management also extends to device mobility and dynamic IP address assignment. In modern networks, especially those with mobile devices like smartphones, laptops, and tablets, it is essential to ensure that these devices can connect to the network seamlessly as they move between different locations. DHCP enables this mobility by automatically assigning IP addresses to devices as they join the network, regardless of their physical location. This flexibility is particularly important in environments such as enterprise networks or large campuses, where devices may frequently change locations and need to be dynamically reconfigured.

Ultimately, the integration of DHCP into a configuration management strategy significantly simplifies the process of managing network devices and their configurations. By automating the assignment of IP addresses and network settings, DHCP reduces administrative overhead, improves network reliability, and enhances security by ensuring that devices are consistently and correctly configured. As networks continue to grow in size and complexity, DHCP remains an essential component of an effective configuration management strategy, allowing administrators to efficiently manage large, dynamic networks while ensuring seamless communication and optimal performance.

The Evolution of Configuration Management Protocols

The field of network management has undergone significant transformations over the years, particularly with the rise of configuration management protocols that allow network administrators to efficiently and securely manage the configurations of network devices. These protocols have evolved in response to the increasing complexity and scale of modern networks, the need for automation, and the demand for enhanced security. As organizations expand and rely more heavily on technology, configuration management protocols have adapted to meet the evolving needs of network management. From early, manual processes to sophisticated, automated tools, the evolution of these protocols highlights the growing importance of network configuration in ensuring smooth, secure, and efficient network operations.

The first generation of configuration management protocols emerged in the early days of computer networking. Initially, network devices were manually configured using static methods, where administrators would physically access each device and input configurations directly. As networks grew in size, this manual approach became increasingly impractical, particularly when it came to managing configurations for hundreds or thousands of devices. This led to the development of the first protocols designed to automate the configuration process. Early examples included protocols such as the File Transfer Protocol (FTP), which, although not specifically designed for configuration management, provided a way to transfer files between devices over a network. FTP was soon employed to move configuration files to network devices, reducing the need for manual input but still lacking the security features necessary for safe operation in a more connected world.

As the need for more secure and efficient configuration management grew, particularly with the rise of the internet and larger corporate networks, new protocols were developed. The advent of the Dynamic Host Configuration Protocol (DHCP) marked a significant turning point in the evolution of configuration management. DHCP automated the assignment of IP addresses and other network settings, greatly simplifying the task of managing large numbers of devices. Instead of manually assigning IP addresses to each device, network administrators could configure a central DHCP server to dynamically assign IP addresses and other configuration details, ensuring that devices could automatically join the network and be properly configured without manual intervention. This automation was a crucial step toward making network management more scalable and efficient, as it reduced the administrative burden and eliminated errors associated with manual IP address assignment.

While DHCP made significant strides in simplifying network configuration, the need for more secure file transfer methods led to the development of the Secure Copy Protocol (SCP). SCP was built on top of the Secure Shell (SSH) protocol, which was originally designed to provide secure remote login capabilities. SCP allowed network administrators to securely transfer configuration files, scripts, and other data between devices, ensuring that sensitive information was encrypted during transfer. SCP became an essential protocol for configuration management, especially in environments where security was paramount. As the internet grew and cyber threats became more prevalent, the need for secure file transfers led to the widespread adoption of SCP, which ensured that configuration files could be transferred without exposing them to unauthorized access or tampering.

The next evolution in configuration management protocols came with the introduction of the Simple Network Management Protocol (SNMP). SNMP provided a standardized method for monitoring and managing network devices, such as routers, switches, and firewalls. Unlike earlier protocols, which focused primarily on file transfer and configuration updates, SNMP offered real-time monitoring and management capabilities, allowing administrators to gather performance data, configure devices, and troubleshoot issues from a centralized location. SNMP's ability to provide insight into device health, performance metrics, and network status made it a crucial tool for network administrators. It also enabled more sophisticated approaches to configuration management, as administrators could remotely manage devices, adjust configurations, and ensure that devices were operating within specified parameters.

As networks became increasingly complex and diverse, the need for more comprehensive and automated configuration management solutions grew. In response, newer protocols and tools were developed to address the challenges of managing modern, dynamic networks. The introduction of the Configuration Management Database (CMDB) and tools like Puppet, Chef, and Ansible revolutionized the way administrators manage network configurations. These modern tools go beyond simply transferring files or updating device settings; they enable infrastructure as code (IaC), where network configurations are defined and managed programmatically. This allows administrators to automate the deployment, configuration, and monitoring of network devices across large-scale networks, all while ensuring consistency and reducing the risk of human error. Tools like Ansible, for example, allow administrators to define network configurations in simple YAML files, which are then automatically deployed to devices. This shift toward automation has greatly increased the efficiency and scalability of configuration management processes, making it easier to manage complex network environments.

With the growth of cloud computing and virtualization, configuration management protocols have continued to evolve to accommodate these new technologies. Virtual networks, cloud services, and containerized environments present unique challenges in terms of configuration management, as they involve rapidly changing infrastructure and dynamic environments. In response, configuration management tools have adapted to support the needs of modern IT infrastructure. Cloud platforms like Amazon Web Services (AWS) and Microsoft Azure have introduced their own configuration management services, such as AWS Systems Manager and Azure Automation, which allow administrators to manage configurations across hybrid and multi-cloud environments. These services integrate with existing tools and protocols like Ansible, Terraform, and Puppet, offering more flexibility in managing cloud-based and on-premises devices from a single interface.

At the same time, the rise of network automation tools has pushed the boundaries of configuration management even further. Network automation frameworks such as Cisco's Digital Network Architecture (DNA), Juniper's Contrail, and VMware's NSX offer integrated platforms that automate both the configuration and monitoring of network devices. These platforms use advanced protocols and software-defined networking (SDN) principles to dynamically configure and manage network devices, allowing for real-time changes to configurations without manual intervention. Automation frameworks like these not only simplify configuration management but also enable more efficient and resilient network operations, as changes to configurations can be tested and deployed automatically, reducing the risk of misconfiguration and network downtime.

The continuous evolution of configuration management protocols reflects the growing complexity of network environments and the increasing need for security, automation, and scalability. Today's networks are highly dynamic, with a mix of physical, virtual, and cloud-based devices. Modern configuration management protocols must be able to support this diversity while maintaining the security, consistency, and efficiency that administrators require. Whether it's through automating IP address assignments with DHCP, securely transferring configuration files with SCP, or leveraging advanced network automation platforms, the role of configuration management protocols continues to evolve in response to the ever-changing demands of modern IT infrastructure. As networks continue to grow and become more intricate, these protocols will remain essential for ensuring the smooth, secure, and efficient operation of network systems.

The Role of HTTPS in Configuration Management Security

As organizations increasingly rely on digital infrastructure, securing configuration management processes has become a critical priority. Network devices, software configurations, and system settings often contain sensitive information that, if compromised, could lead to significant security risks. The use of Hypertext Transfer Protocol Secure (HTTPS) has become a foundational component of securing configuration management, as it provides a secure means of communication over the internet. By ensuring that data is encrypted during transmission and that identity verification is robust, HTTPS plays an essential role in maintaining the integrity and confidentiality of configuration files and other critical system information.

At its core, HTTPS is an extension of the standard Hypertext Transfer Protocol (HTTP), which is the protocol used for web communication. Unlike HTTP, HTTPS uses Transport Layer Security (TLS) or its predecessor, Secure Sockets Layer (SSL), to encrypt the data exchanged between the client and server. This encryption ensures that any sensitive information, such as login credentials, configuration settings, and other critical data, is protected from interception during transmission. When applied to configuration management, HTTPS ensures that configuration files and system settings are not exposed to unauthorized parties during the transfer process, which is especially important when those files are transferred over public or untrusted networks.

Configuration management often involves the need to securely transmit configuration files, scripts, and system updates between management systems, network devices, and administrators. These transfers are typically performed through web-based interfaces or RESTful APIs, and HTTPS provides the necessary security to protect the data in transit. Without HTTPS, configuration data could be transmitted in plain text, making it vulnerable to interception by attackers using man-in-the-middle (MITM) attacks or other methods of eavesdropping. For example, an attacker intercepting a configuration file transfer could potentially alter the file, insert malicious code, or steal sensitive information, putting the network and its users at risk. HTTPS prevents such attacks by ensuring that the communication is encrypted and that the identity of the parties involved is authenticated.

In addition to providing encryption, HTTPS also includes mechanisms for server authentication. In a configuration management system, this means that the client can verify the identity of the server it is communicating with before transmitting any sensitive information. This is achieved through the use of digital certificates, which are issued by trusted certificate authorities (CAs). When a server presents its certificate, the client can verify its authenticity by checking the certificate against a trusted CA's root certificates. This authentication process helps to prevent attackers from impersonating a legitimate server and gaining access to sensitive configuration data. By ensuring that the server is legitimate, HTTPS adds an extra layer of trust to the configuration management process, ensuring that administrators are interacting with the correct systems and not malicious entities.

The role of HTTPS in configuration management security extends to web-based management platforms as well. Many modern configuration management systems, whether they are used for managing network devices, servers, or cloud infrastructure, rely on web-based interfaces for administrators to make changes, view configurations, and deploy updates. These platforms often require authentication and the exchange of sensitive data, including passwords, access tokens, and configuration files. Without HTTPS, these interactions would be highly susceptible to interception and exploitation. By using HTTPS, web-based management platforms can ensure that the transmission of sensitive information is encrypted and that administrators' login credentials and actions are secure. This is especially important for cloud-based or remotely accessible systems where attackers might exploit vulnerabilities in less secure protocols.

In addition to encryption and authentication, HTTPS also supports data integrity. When transferring configuration files or updates, it is essential that the data received by the recipient matches the data sent by the sender. HTTPS ensures that the data is not altered in transit by using message authentication codes (MACs) as part of the encryption process. If the data is tampered with during transmission, the MAC will no longer match, and the recipient can detect that the data has been altered. This feature is especially important in configuration management because even small changes to configuration files can lead to unintended consequences, such as system failures, security vulnerabilities, or misconfigurations. HTTPS provides a means to verify that the configuration data is intact and has not been modified during transfer, reducing the risk of these issues.

HTTPS also plays an essential role in the broader security ecosystem by supporting the use of secure APIs for configuration management automation. As organizations increasingly adopt DevOps practices and automate their infrastructure management, RESTful APIs have become a common method for interacting with configuration management systems. These APIs often require the transmission of sensitive data, including configuration files, access tokens, and authentication credentials. By using HTTPS, these API communications are encrypted, ensuring that sensitive data is protected from interception. Additionally, the authentication provided by HTTPS ensures that only authorized clients can interact with the configuration management system, preventing unauthorized access and potential breaches.

The importance of HTTPS in configuration management security extends beyond individual transfers of configuration files or API calls. In larger, more complex network environments, configuration management often involves multiple systems working in tandem to ensure that devices and services are properly configured, updated, and secured. HTTPS ensures that these systems can securely communicate with each other, exchanging configuration information and updates without exposing the data to potential attackers. Whether it is syncing configurations across multiple servers, deploying updates to remote devices, or interacting with cloud services, HTTPS ensures that the communication between these systems remains secure and protected.

Furthermore, the adoption of HTTPS in configuration management is an essential component of compliance with various industry standards and regulations. Many regulatory frameworks, such as the General Data Protection Regulation (GDPR), the Health Insurance Portability and Accountability Act (HIPAA), and the Payment Card Industry Data Security Standard (PCI DSS), require organizations to protect sensitive data during transmission. Using HTTPS ensures that organizations comply with these regulations by encrypting data in transit and protecting it from unauthorized access. By incorporating HTTPS into their configuration management practices, organizations can meet regulatory requirements and avoid penalties or legal issues related to data security.

As network environments become more complex and the need for secure communication grows, HTTPS will continue to play a critical role in configuration management security. Its ability to provide encryption, authentication, and data integrity makes it an essential tool for ensuring the safe transfer of sensitive configuration data. In an era where cyber threats are increasingly sophisticated, HTTPS offers a robust and reliable means of securing configuration management processes, enabling administrators to confidently manage and update network devices and systems without exposing them to unnecessary risks. By leveraging HTTPS in configuration management, organizations can maintain a secure, reliable, and compliant network environment that supports the growing demands of modern digital infrastructure.

Advanced File Transfer Techniques: Using Rsync for Configuration Management

In the world of network and system administration, the need to efficiently manage and transfer configuration files, backups, and updates across multiple systems is a critical task. Traditional methods such as FTP or SCP are widely used, but as networks become larger and more complex, more advanced file transfer techniques are needed. One such technique is Rsync, a powerful and efficient tool that has gained widespread adoption for file synchronization and transfer. Rsync's ability to perform incremental transfers, preserve file attributes, and ensure reliability makes it an excellent choice for configuration management in dynamic and distributed environments.

Rsync, short for Remote Synchronization, is a file transfer and synchronization tool that was initially developed for Unix-like systems but is now available on a variety of platforms. What sets Rsync apart from other file transfer protocols is its ability to only transfer the differences between source and destination files. This makes Rsync highly efficient, especially when dealing with large files or directories, as it minimizes the amount of data that needs to be transmitted. Instead of copying an entire file, Rsync compares the source and destination, calculates the differences, and only sends the changes. This incremental transfer method can significantly reduce both the time and bandwidth required for file transfers, making it an ideal choice for configuration management in environments where updates and changes are frequent.

In configuration management, Rsync's ability to synchronize files between multiple systems is particularly useful. For example, when managing the configuration files of multiple servers or network devices, it is often necessary to ensure that each device has the latest configuration or update. Manually updating each device can be a time-consuming and error-prone process, especially when there are many devices in the network. Rsync can automate this process by enabling administrators to sync configuration files between a central repository and remote devices quickly and efficiently. By setting up Rsync to run on a scheduled basis, administrators can ensure that configuration files are regularly updated, without the need for manual intervention.

Rsync also provides a variety of options that make it highly customizable for configuration management tasks. One of the key features of Rsync is its ability to preserve file attributes such as permissions, ownership, timestamps, and symbolic links. This is particularly important when managing configuration files, as ensuring that the integrity of file attributes is maintained is essential for proper system operation. For example, when transferring configuration files for a web server or database server, it is critical that the file permissions and ownership are preserved to ensure that the system continues to function securely and as expected. With Rsync, administrators can specify options to preserve these attributes during the transfer process, ensuring that the configurations are not only synchronized but also retain their integrity.

Another important feature of Rsync is its ability to compress data during transfer, which can be particularly useful when working with large configuration files or when operating in bandwidth-constrained environments. By using Rsync's built-in compression feature, administrators can reduce the amount of data transmitted over the network, leading to faster file transfers and reduced bandwidth consumption. This is especially beneficial in remote environments, where network latency and limited bandwidth can be significant concerns. Compression can help mitigate these issues, ensuring that configuration updates or backups are completed in a timely and efficient manner.

Rsync is also highly versatile in terms of the ways it can be used for configuration management. It supports both local and remote transfers, allowing files to be synchronized between local directories on a single system, or between a local system and a remote server. This makes it useful not only for transferring configuration files between servers but also for backing up configuration files from remote devices to a central server. By automating the backup process with Rsync, administrators can ensure that configuration files are regularly backed up, providing a reliable means of disaster recovery. If a device or system experiences a failure or requires a rollback to a previous configuration, the backup files can be quickly restored using Rsync, minimizing downtime and restoring system functionality.

Rsync also supports synchronization across multiple devices, which is especially useful in large-scale environments. For instance, if an organization manages hundreds or thousands of devices, manually updating each configuration file can be overwhelming. With Rsync, administrators can set up synchronization between a central configuration repository and all remote devices, ensuring that each system is automatically updated with the latest configurations. Rsync can be run as a cron job or scheduled task, allowing for regular synchronization without manual intervention. This automation not only saves time but also ensures consistency across the entire network, reducing the risk of errors and discrepancies between devices.

Security is another key consideration in configuration management, and Rsync offers several options for securing file transfers. By using Rsync over SSH (Secure Shell), administrators can ensure that file transfers are encrypted, preventing unauthorized access to sensitive configuration files. SSH provides strong encryption, ensuring that data is protected from eavesdropping or tampering during transfer. Additionally, Rsync supports the use of SSH key authentication, which eliminates the need for passwords and provides a more secure and automated means of authentication. By leveraging SSH and Rsync's robust security features, administrators can safely synchronize configuration files across networks, even in untrusted environments.

Despite its many advantages, there are certain considerations to keep in mind when using Rsync for configuration management. While Rsync is highly efficient, it can be resource-intensive when working with large volumes of data, especially on systems with limited processing power or bandwidth. It is important for administrators to carefully plan the timing and frequency of Rsync operations to avoid overwhelming system resources or network bandwidth. Additionally, Rsync's incremental transfer feature works by comparing files on the source and destination, which can sometimes result in issues if files are modified externally or in unexpected ways. In such cases, administrators should ensure that the synchronization process is carefully monitored and that any conflicts or discrepancies are addressed promptly.

Rsync's powerful features and flexibility make it an indispensable tool in configuration management, especially for environments where efficiency, security, and automation are critical. Its ability to perform incremental file transfers, preserve file attributes, compress data, and synchronize files across multiple systems makes it well-suited for automating the management of configuration files and system updates. When integrated into configuration management workflows, Rsync can significantly reduce the time and effort required to maintain and update systems, while ensuring that configuration files remain consistent, secure, and reliable. With its robust security features and versatility, Rsync continues to play a vital role in the effective management of modern networks and systems.

Integrating Configuration Management Protocols with Network Monitoring Tools

In the ever-evolving landscape of network management, ensuring that configurations are properly maintained, synchronized, and up-to-date across devices is vital for network stability and performance. Configuration management protocols such as TFTP, SCP, and SFTP play a pivotal role in automating and securing the transfer and management of configuration files. However, to truly optimize network operations, these protocols need to be integrated with network monitoring tools. By combining configuration management protocols with monitoring solutions, administrators can achieve a more comprehensive, responsive, and efficient approach to network management. This integration ensures that network configurations are not only managed properly but also continuously monitored for performance, security, and compliance.

Network monitoring tools are essential for tracking the health and performance of network devices, servers, and infrastructure. These tools collect and analyze data on network traffic, device status, resource utilization, and other key performance indicators (KPIs). With the integration of configuration management protocols, administrators can gain deeper insights into how configuration changes affect network performance. For example, when a new configuration is deployed using SCP or TFTP, network monitoring tools can track the impact of those changes on network traffic, device responsiveness, and uptime. This allows administrators to quickly identify any issues that arise from configuration updates, such as performance degradation, errors, or security vulnerabilities, and take corrective action.

One of the key benefits of integrating configuration management protocols with network monitoring tools is the ability to automate the configuration deployment process while simultaneously monitoring the results. Network monitoring tools can be configured to automatically alert administrators whenever a configuration change is made, or when a new device is added to the network. These alerts can help ensure that administrators are aware of all configuration changes in real-time, providing them with the ability to monitor the success or failure of configuration updates. Additionally, network monitoring tools can provide insights into how these changes affect network performance. For instance, if a new firewall configuration leads to increased latency or a network bottleneck, monitoring tools can immediately notify the administrator of the issue, allowing for rapid troubleshooting and resolution.

Furthermore, integrating configuration management protocols with monitoring tools enhances security by providing visibility into potential vulnerabilities. Configuration errors or misconfigurations are often the root cause of network security breaches. By linking configuration management tools like SCP or TFTP with monitoring solutions, administrators can not only deploy configurations but also continuously monitor their security posture. Network monitoring tools can track changes to configurations and detect any unauthorized modifications or discrepancies. If a configuration file is altered without authorization, the monitoring system can send an alert to administrators, enabling them to respond quickly and mitigate any potential risks.

Network monitoring tools also help verify the accuracy and consistency of configuration deployments across devices. In large-scale networks, ensuring that every device has the correct configuration is crucial for maintaining uniformity and preventing configuration drift. Configuration management protocols like SCP enable administrators to deploy standardized configuration files, but monitoring tools help ensure that these configurations are consistently applied across the network. Through ongoing monitoring, administrators can confirm that the devices are receiving the correct configurations, and they can detect devices that may not have received the latest updates due to network issues or failures. This verification process helps maintain configuration integrity and avoids operational disruptions caused by misconfigured devices.

Integration with network monitoring tools also facilitates troubleshooting and problem resolution. When a configuration change leads to network instability or degraded performance, the monitoring system can provide valuable diagnostic information. By analyzing metrics such as packet loss, latency, and device health, administrators can pinpoint the specific cause of the issue, whether it's a configuration error, a network failure, or a performance bottleneck. For example, if a network switch is not responding correctly after a configuration update, monitoring tools can help identify the underlying cause, such as a mismatch in VLAN settings or an incorrect routing configuration. This enables administrators to fix the issue faster, minimizing downtime and ensuring the network remains operational.

Additionally, integrating configuration management protocols with network monitoring tools offers valuable insights into compliance management. Many industries require that network configurations adhere to specific standards and regulatory requirements, such as those set by PCI-DSS, HIPAA, or GDPR. Through integration, administrators can use monitoring tools to ensure that configuration files are compliant with these standards. For example, network monitoring tools can track whether security-related configuration settings, such as encryption protocols or access controls, are properly configured on all devices. If a device falls out of compliance, the monitoring system can flag the issue, prompting administrators to review the configuration and make necessary changes.

Another significant advantage of integrating configuration management with monitoring is the ability to audit configuration changes over time. Network monitoring tools can keep a history of all configuration changes, including who made the changes, when they occurred, and what was modified. This audit trail is crucial for tracking the evolution of the network's configuration and ensuring accountability. In the event of a network incident or security breach, having access to detailed logs of configuration changes helps administrators identify potential points of failure and understand how the network was impacted. This historical record of changes can also be useful for compliance audits, as it provides proof that network configurations have been properly managed and monitored.

The integration of configuration management protocols and network monitoring tools also streamlines network automation. In modern IT environments, network automation is essential for managing complex, dynamic systems. By combining configuration management with monitoring solutions, administrators can automate not just the deployment of configurations, but also the monitoring and correction of configurations in real-time. Automation tools can detect when a device falls out of compliance or a configuration change leads to undesirable consequences, and they can automatically trigger corrective actions, such as reapplying a previous configuration, restarting a device, or alerting an administrator. This automated response ensures that network issues are addressed quickly and that configurations are consistently enforced across the network.

Relying on integration between configuration management protocols and network monitoring tools also fosters proactive management. Instead of waiting for issues to arise, administrators can use monitoring data to predict potential problems and take preventative measures. For example, by analyzing trends in network traffic, device performance, and configuration stability, administrators can identify areas of concern before they become critical issues. By automating configuration updates and combining this with continuous monitoring, administrators can stay ahead of potential problems and ensure that the network operates smoothly and efficiently.

By integrating configuration management protocols with network monitoring tools, network administrators can achieve a comprehensive, automated, and secure approach to network management. This integration enables seamless configuration updates, real-time monitoring, and rapid response to issues, ensuring that devices are always properly configured and performing optimally. It also strengthens security, compliance, and troubleshooting capabilities, providing administrators with the insights they need to maintain a healthy, reliable network infrastructure. Through this integration, organizations can optimize network operations, reduce downtime, and improve the overall efficiency and effectiveness of their network management processes.

Building a Secure File Transfer Framework with SCP, TFTP, and Beyond

In today's highly connected world, managing and securing file transfers is crucial for maintaining the integrity, availability, and confidentiality of data. Whether it's configuration files, system updates, or sensitive information, securely transferring files across networks is a fundamental task in IT management. As networks grow in complexity and scale, building a secure file transfer framework becomes essential. Various protocols, such as Secure Copy Protocol (SCP), Trivial File Transfer Protocol (TFTP), and others, each offer different features and benefits that can be used to address specific security and operational requirements. A well-rounded approach that integrates these protocols, when used appropriately, can provide both security and efficiency, forming the foundation of an effective file transfer framework.

The SCP protocol is one of the cornerstones of secure file transfers in modern networks. Built on top of the Secure Shell (SSH) protocol, SCP ensures that file transfers are encrypted and authenticated. The encryption provided by SSH protects the data being transmitted from eavesdropping or tampering, making SCP a highly secure option for transferring files over potentially untrusted networks. SCP is particularly useful when transferring sensitive configuration files, backup data, or software updates, as it ensures that these files remain confidential and intact during transmission. By utilizing SCP, administrators can avoid the risks associated with plaintext transfer protocols, such as FTP, which expose sensitive data to interception.

One of the key advantages of SCP is its simplicity and efficiency. SCP allows for secure file transfers with minimal configuration, which is ideal for network administrators who need a straightforward, no-fuss solution for secure data transmission. The protocol operates over a single encrypted connection, ensuring that both the control and data channels are secure. SCP also allows for easy automation through scripts, which makes it an excellent choice for regular tasks like configuration backups or firmware updates. With automated SCP transfers, administrators can ensure that critical files are securely transferred at regular intervals without manual intervention, improving both security and operational efficiency.

While SCP provides a secure method for file transfer, its reliance on SSH means it is best suited for environments where security is the primary concern. In contrast, TFTP is a lightweight protocol that is often used in environments where security is less of a concern, and speed is prioritized over encryption. TFTP operates over the User Datagram Protocol (UDP), which does not include the error correction and acknowledgment features of the Transmission Control Protocol (TCP). As a result, TFTP is faster and consumes fewer resources compared to SCP, making it an excellent choice for transferring small configuration files or boot images in trusted, isolated networks. TFTP is commonly used in scenarios like network booting, where devices need to retrieve boot images or firmware files quickly from a centralized server.

However, while TFTP offers speed and simplicity, it does so at the expense of security. TFTP does not provide any encryption or authentication mechanisms, which makes it vulnerable to man-in-the-middle attacks and eavesdropping. Therefore, TFTP should only be used in controlled environments where the risk of unauthorized access is minimal, and the data being transferred is not sensitive. When used in combination with other secure protocols, TFTP can be part of a larger secure file transfer framework that balances speed and security.

To build a secure file transfer framework, organizations should also consider integrating additional security measures such as Virtual Private Networks (VPNs) or secure tunnels. By combining protocols like SCP and TFTP with VPNs, administrators can ensure that file transfers are protected from interception even in untrusted environments. VPNs encrypt all traffic between the client and server, adding an additional layer of security on top of the encryption provided by SCP or TFTP. This layered approach to security is particularly beneficial in scenarios where devices must be accessed remotely or across public networks, ensuring that sensitive files remain protected regardless of the transfer protocol being used.

Another option for securing file transfers is the use of File Transfer Protocol Secure (FTPS) or Secure File Transfer Protocol (SFTP). Both protocols provide enhanced security compared to standard FTP, using SSL/TLS encryption to protect data during transmission. FTPS and SFTP both offer secure channels for transferring files, but they operate differently. FTPS is an extension of FTP that adds SSL/TLS support, while SFTP is a completely different protocol built on top of SSH. SFTP, like SCP, ensures that both the data and control channels are encrypted and provides robust authentication through SSH keys or passwords. Depending on the specific use case, either FTPS or SFTP can be integrated into a secure file transfer framework for environments where FTP is preferred, but encryption and secure authentication are required.

When designing a secure file transfer framework, administrators must also consider aspects such as access control and monitoring. Even the most secure transfer protocols can be compromised if access control is not properly enforced. A robust file transfer framework should include mechanisms to authenticate users before allowing them to access or transfer files. This can be achieved by using SSH keys, certificates, or multi-factor authentication (MFA) to ensure that only authorized individuals can initiate transfers. Additionally, all file transfers should be logged and monitored for auditing purposes. By tracking who accessed which files and when, administrators can identify potential security incidents or policy violations early on and take appropriate corrective actions.

The integration of automated monitoring tools can further enhance the security and efficiency of a file transfer framework. Automated tools can be used to detect anomalies in file transfer activities, such as unauthorized access attempts, unusual transfer patterns, or failed login attempts. By setting up alerts and notifications, administrators can be immediately informed of any suspicious activity and take action to prevent security breaches. These tools can also be configured to automatically enforce security policies, such as blocking transfers to certain locations or users, based on predefined rules.

As part of a larger security strategy, encryption should be a key consideration for all file transfer protocols. While protocols like SCP, SFTP, and FTPS inherently provide encryption, administrators must ensure that proper encryption standards are enforced at all levels. This includes ensuring that strong encryption algorithms are used, keys are managed securely, and the encryption standards comply with industry regulations and best practices. Regular key rotation and the use of strong encryption keys are essential to maintaining the security of file transfers over time.

The integration of SCP, TFTP, SFTP, and other secure file transfer protocols with monitoring tools, encryption standards, and robust access control policies can provide a comprehensive framework for managing configuration files and other sensitive data securely. By combining these protocols with best practices for encryption, authentication, and monitoring, administrators can build a file transfer system that ensures both efficiency and security. Whether it is updating configuration files, transferring backups, or deploying software updates, a well-designed file transfer framework is essential for maintaining the integrity, confidentiality, and availability of critical system information across modern networks.

The Role of Configuration Management in Software Deployment

In the fast-paced world of IT infrastructure management, the deployment of software applications across multiple systems is a crucial task that must be done efficiently and reliably. Configuration management plays a central role in this process, providing a structured and automated approach to managing the configurations of the systems involved in software deployment. By ensuring that systems are configured correctly, uniformly, and securely, configuration management ensures that software deployment processes are streamlined and that the deployment is consistent across all environments. Without effective configuration management, software deployment can become chaotic, error-prone, and time-consuming, particularly in large-scale, dynamic environments.

At its core, configuration management in software deployment is about ensuring that all systems involved in the deployment process are correctly configured to support the installation, execution, and integration of the software. This involves managing the settings, parameters, and configurations of the servers, workstations, or cloud environments that the software will run on. For instance, deploying a new version of a web application might involve ensuring that the correct server settings, environment variables, and system dependencies are in place across multiple machines. Configuration management tools can automate these tasks, reducing the need for manual configuration and ensuring consistency across the systems involved.

One of the key benefits of configuration management in software deployment is automation. In modern IT environments, particularly in DevOps and continuous integration/continuous deployment (CI/CD) workflows, automation is essential for managing the speed and complexity of software deployment. Configuration management tools like Ansible, Puppet, and Chef enable administrators to automate the process of configuring systems to prepare them for software deployment. By defining configurations as code, these tools allow administrators to specify exactly how the software should be installed, configured, and maintained across all systems in a repeatable and predictable manner. This approach minimizes human intervention and the risk of errors that could result in inconsistent deployments.

Automation also helps improve the speed and reliability of software deployments. By automating the configuration of the systems involved, configuration management tools allow software to be deployed faster and with fewer disruptions. This is particularly important in large-scale environments where manual configuration of each machine would be too time-consuming and error-prone. Instead of manually configuring each system, administrators can write configuration scripts or playbooks that specify exactly how the systems should be set up. These scripts can then be executed automatically across multiple systems, ensuring that each system is configured correctly before the software is deployed. This not only speeds up the deployment process but also ensures that the deployment is done in a consistent and reliable manner.

Consistency is another crucial aspect of software deployment that configuration management addresses. When deploying software to multiple systems, particularly in large, distributed environments, it is essential that all systems are configured in the same way to avoid incompatibilities and configuration drift. Configuration drift occurs when the configurations of different systems become inconsistent over time, which can lead to errors and failures when deploying or running software. By using configuration management tools, administrators can ensure that all systems are configured uniformly, reducing the chances of drift and ensuring that software is deployed in a stable and predictable environment.

Another important role of configuration management in software deployment is managing system dependencies. Many software applications require specific versions of libraries, packages, or other software components to function correctly. If these dependencies are not properly managed, the software may fail to install or run correctly. Configuration management tools can help ensure that all necessary dependencies are installed and configured correctly before the software is deployed. For example, a configuration management tool can check that the correct version of a database or a runtime environment is installed on each machine and can automatically install or update the necessary components as part of the deployment process. This ensures that the software has the necessary environment to run successfully and reduces the chances of deployment failures caused by missing or incompatible dependencies.

Security is another critical concern in software deployment, and configuration management plays a vital role in securing the systems involved in the deployment process. Configuration management tools allow administrators to enforce security best practices, such as ensuring that systems are up to date with the latest patches, using secure communication protocols, and limiting access to critical resources. For example, configuration management can ensure that only authorized users have access to the deployment scripts, that firewall settings are correctly configured, and that the systems have the latest security patches installed before deploying the software. This helps to prevent security vulnerabilities that could be exploited during the deployment process, ensuring that the software is deployed securely and that the systems remain protected throughout the deployment lifecycle.

In addition to security, configuration management also plays a key role in monitoring and auditing software deployments. By keeping track of configuration changes and deployment processes, administrators can maintain an audit trail that provides valuable insights into the deployment process. This is particularly important in environments that require compliance with regulatory standards, such as financial institutions, healthcare providers, or government agencies. Configuration management tools can generate logs of all configuration changes and deployment activities, which can then be reviewed to ensure that the deployment process is in compliance with relevant regulations and policies. These logs can also be used for troubleshooting purposes, helping administrators identify and resolve issues that arise during the deployment process.

Furthermore, configuration management facilitates the rollback of software deployments in the event of failure. In any deployment process, there is always a risk that something may go wrong, whether it's a software bug, an unexpected system incompatibility, or an error in the configuration process. Configuration management tools can help mitigate this risk by enabling administrators to quickly and easily roll back to a previous, known good configuration. This ensures that the software deployment process is not only faster and more reliable but also safer, as administrators can quickly recover from any issues that arise during deployment.

The role of configuration management in software deployment also extends to cloud-based environments. With the increasing adoption of cloud computing, organizations are deploying software across a mix of on-premises and cloud-based systems. Configuration management tools allow administrators to manage configurations across hybrid environments, ensuring that software is deployed consistently and securely across both on-premises servers and cloud instances. This enables organizations to maintain flexibility and scalability while ensuring that all systems are configured correctly, regardless of where they are hosted.

By leveraging configuration management in software deployment, organizations can ensure that their deployment processes are more efficient, consistent, and secure. Automation, dependency management, security enforcement, and auditing are just a few of the ways that configuration management enhances the deployment process. Whether it's for traditional infrastructure, cloud environments, or hybrid systems, configuration management plays a central role in enabling faster, more reliable, and more secure software deployments, helping organizations stay competitive and operational in an increasingly complex digital landscape.

Using Version Control Systems in Network Configuration Management

The complexity of modern networks, combined with the need for consistent, secure, and reliable configurations across a wide array of devices, makes effective configuration management crucial. As networks scale and evolve, the challenge of tracking changes to network device configurations becomes increasingly difficult. Without a systematic approach, configuration errors can lead to network disruptions, security vulnerabilities, and costly downtime. One of the most effective ways to manage network configurations and ensure the integrity of network devices is by using version control systems (VCS). These systems, traditionally used in software development, provide powerful tools to track, manage, and revert changes to configurations, ensuring that network administrators can maintain stable, secure, and consistent configurations across all devices.

Version control systems, such as Git, Subversion, or Mercurial, allow network administrators to manage the evolution of configuration files over time. Just as version control systems track changes in source code, they can also track changes in network configurations, providing a detailed record of who made the changes, what changes were made, and when they were made. This historical record is invaluable when troubleshooting issues, recovering from configuration errors, or auditing network configurations for compliance with security policies or regulatory requirements. By leveraging VCS in network configuration management, administrators can gain greater visibility into the configuration process, ensuring that configurations are applied consistently and securely across all devices.

One of the main benefits of using a version control system in network configuration management is the ability to maintain multiple versions of configuration files. In dynamic network environments, configurations are constantly changing as new devices are added, software is updated, or network policies are modified. Managing these changes manually is error-prone and can result in misconfigurations that cause network failures. By using a VCS, administrators can easily track different versions of a configuration file, allowing them to roll back to a previous version if a configuration change causes issues. For instance, if a new routing configuration leads to network outages, administrators can quickly revert to a known working configuration using the version control system, minimizing downtime and reducing the impact of errors.

Version control also provides a way to manage collaborative configuration management. In large organizations or distributed teams, multiple administrators may need to make changes to the same network configuration files. Without a version control system, coordinating these changes can be difficult, and conflicts can arise when two administrators try to modify the same configuration file simultaneously. A VCS resolves these issues by allowing administrators to work on different branches of the configuration file, merging their changes when necessary. This way, changes can be tracked individually, and conflicts can be resolved automatically or manually, ensuring that the final configuration is stable and reliable. Furthermore, using a VCS enables administrators to establish workflows where configuration changes are reviewed and approved before being applied, adding an extra layer of control to the process.

Another important advantage of using version control in network configuration management is the ability to document changes effectively. In traditional network management, configuration changes are often made on the fly without a detailed record of why the change was made or what its intended effects were. This lack of documentation can make troubleshooting difficult and can lead to confusion when trying to understand the reasoning behind past configuration changes. With a version control system, each change can be associated with a commit message, providing context and explanations for why a change was made. This documentation is especially useful for auditing purposes, as it helps track the decision-making process behind configuration changes, ensuring that network configurations align with organizational goals and security standards.

Integrating version control systems with automation tools further enhances network configuration management. In modern network environments, automation is critical for managing the growing number of devices and configurations. Tools such as Ansible, Puppet, or Chef can be integrated with a version control system to automate the deployment of configuration changes across devices. By storing configuration files in a VCS, administrators can use these automation tools to automatically push changes to network devices, ensuring that configurations are updated consistently and without error. The version control system serves as the central repository for all configuration files, allowing administrators to track changes and deploy updates in a controlled, predictable manner. This integration not only improves efficiency but also ensures that configurations are managed securely, reducing the risk of human error.

Moreover, version control systems allow for better disaster recovery and business continuity. In the event of a network failure or security incident, being able to quickly restore a previous configuration is critical for minimizing downtime and ensuring service continuity. With a VCS, administrators can restore configurations to a known good state in just a few steps. Whether it's recovering from a misconfiguration, a security breach, or a hardware failure, the version history provides a safety net, allowing administrators to quickly roll back to a working configuration. This ability to revert configurations ensures that networks can recover rapidly from unforeseen issues, minimizing disruptions and ensuring that critical services remain operational.

Using version control systems also helps enforce best practices in network configuration management. By maintaining all configuration files in a central, version-controlled repository, organizations can ensure that configurations are stored in a secure and organized manner. Access to the configuration files can be tightly controlled through permissions, ensuring that only authorized administrators can make changes. Additionally, VCS provides an audit trail of who made each change, when it was made, and what was changed, which can be invaluable for compliance purposes. This traceability helps organizations meet security standards and regulatory requirements, ensuring that network configurations are compliant with industry best practices.

Another advantage of using version control in network configuration management is the ability to perform comparisons between different configuration versions. As networks evolve, administrators often need to compare configurations to understand what changes have been made and how they may impact the network. A version control system makes this task easy by allowing administrators to view the differences between two versions of a configuration file. This is particularly useful when troubleshooting or validating changes, as it helps identify the exact configuration changes that might have caused a problem or conflict.

In larger, more complex networks, managing configuration files across multiple locations and systems can be a daunting task. Version control systems help streamline this process by providing a centralized platform where all configuration files can be stored, accessed, and managed. This centralized approach makes it easier for administrators to ensure that configurations are applied uniformly across all devices, regardless of their location. Whether the network spans multiple data centers, remote offices, or cloud environments, version control ensures that configuration files are consistent and up-to-date, reducing the risk of errors and ensuring smooth operation.

Ultimately, using version control systems in network configuration management provides numerous benefits that improve the efficiency, security, and reliability of network operations. By providing a systematic way to track, manage, and automate configuration changes, VCS enhances collaboration, simplifies troubleshooting, and supports business continuity. Whether managing a small network or a global infrastructure, version control systems are an indispensable tool for maintaining the stability and security of modern networks.

Remote Configuration Management: A Growing Trend in Network Administration

The landscape of network administration has experienced significant changes over the last few years, driven largely by the increasing demand for flexible, scalable, and efficient network management solutions. Among the most prominent trends in this evolution is the rise of remote configuration management. With the rapid expansion of distributed networks, cloud-based infrastructures, and the growing number of remote workers, network administrators are finding that managing configurations remotely is not only more efficient but also increasingly necessary. Remote configuration management offers numerous benefits, including reduced operational costs, improved scalability, and enhanced flexibility, all of which are crucial for modern network administration.

Traditionally, network administrators managed configurations directly on-site, accessing network devices physically or through secure remote sessions. However, as networks have become more complex and geographically dispersed, this approach has become less viable. The advent of remote configuration management allows administrators to access and manage network devices from virtually anywhere, eliminating the need for constant on-site presence and making network management more adaptable to the modern business environment. The ability to manage network configurations remotely has allowed for significant improvements in response times, resource allocation, and network security, while also addressing challenges associated with managing large-scale networks.

One of the primary advantages of remote configuration management is its ability to streamline administrative tasks. By centralizing control over configuration management and enabling remote access to devices, administrators can make changes to configurations across multiple devices simultaneously, regardless of their physical location. This centralization makes it easier to apply updates, patches, or configuration changes to numerous devices at once, reducing the risk of errors that can occur when making changes manually. Furthermore, the ability to remotely access network devices means that administrators can address issues more quickly, which is especially important in dynamic environments where downtime or misconfigurations can lead to significant disruptions.

In addition to improving efficiency, remote configuration management also facilitates scalability. As organizations grow, their network infrastructure typically becomes more complex, often requiring the management of a larger number of devices spread across various locations. Traditional on-site management methods would require an increasing amount of resources to maintain the network, as administrators would need to travel to different sites or dispatch technicians to physically manage devices. Remote configuration management eliminates this need by providing a way to access and configure devices remotely, regardless of location. This capability is particularly valuable for businesses with distributed networks, branch offices, or global operations, as it allows a centralized team of administrators to manage configurations across a vast network without the need for excessive travel or additional on-site staff.

Another important benefit of remote configuration management is its role in reducing operational costs. With the ability to manage networks remotely, organizations can reduce the need for dedicated on-site IT staff, which can be costly, particularly in large or distributed networks. Remote management allows a smaller team to oversee and manage a larger network, reducing overhead and freeing up resources for other critical tasks. Furthermore, remote configuration management helps eliminate the need for physical infrastructure, such as dedicated management workstations or travel expenses for administrators who would otherwise need to visit different sites. These cost savings can be particularly impactful for small and medium-sized businesses, where budget constraints often make it difficult to invest in the resources required for traditional on-site management.

Security is often cited as a concern with remote access to network devices, but remote configuration management can actually enhance security when implemented properly. By using secure protocols such as Secure Shell (SSH), administrators can access devices remotely with encryption, ensuring that sensitive configuration data is protected during transmission. Additionally, many remote configuration management tools incorporate authentication mechanisms, such as multi-factor authentication (MFA) and role-based access control (RBAC), which ensure that only authorized users can make changes to configurations. By using these secure methods of access, administrators can reduce the risk of unauthorized access to sensitive network configurations while still benefiting from the flexibility of remote management.

Remote configuration management also plays a crucial role in improving disaster recovery and business continuity. In the event of a network failure, natural disaster, or other emergencies, administrators can quickly access and modify configurations to restore services, even if they are not physically present at the affected site. This remote access capability is particularly valuable for organizations that rely on 24/7 network availability, as it allows for rapid response times and minimizes downtime. By having remote access to critical systems, administrators can address issues and restore normal operations without having to wait for technicians to arrive on-site. This ability to manage network configurations remotely also helps organizations meet their recovery time objectives (RTOs) and recovery point objectives (RPOs) in the event of a disaster.

The ability to manage configurations remotely also enables greater flexibility for network administrators. Many organizations today have remote or distributed teams, and the ability to manage network configurations from any location is an essential part of this modern workforce. Whether administrators are working from home, a remote office, or while traveling, remote configuration management ensures that they can access and update network configurations without being tied to a specific location. This flexibility not only improves productivity but also allows organizations to hire and retain top talent, as administrators no longer need to be physically present to perform critical network management tasks.

Cloud computing and virtualization have also contributed significantly to the rise of remote configuration management. As more organizations migrate their infrastructure to the cloud or adopt hybrid environments, the need for centralized and remote management of configurations has become even more pronounced. Cloud-based configuration management tools allow administrators to manage configurations across both on-premises and cloud-based systems from a single interface, providing greater visibility and control over the entire infrastructure. This integration with cloud environments enables administrators to make real-time changes to configurations, ensuring that the network is always operating optimally regardless of whether the resources are hosted in the cloud or on physical servers.

Additionally, as the Internet of Things (IoT) and smart devices proliferate, remote configuration management has become increasingly important. IoT devices, such as network sensors, cameras, and access points, often need to be managed and updated remotely. By using remote configuration management tools, administrators can efficiently manage and configure these devices across large and dispersed networks without the need for on-site intervention. This scalability is essential as the number of connected devices continues to grow, making remote management not only beneficial but essential for maintaining network integrity.

The integration of artificial intelligence (AI) and machine learning (ML) into remote configuration management is another area where the trend is evolving. These technologies can be used to analyze network data, predict potential issues, and automate configuration changes based on real-time network conditions. By leveraging AI and ML, administrators can proactively manage network configurations, identifying problems before they occur and optimizing the network performance without needing constant manual intervention. This level of automation further enhances the flexibility and scalability of remote configuration management, ensuring that networks can be managed more efficiently and securely.

As network infrastructures continue to grow and become more complex, the importance of remote configuration management will only increase. The ability to manage configurations remotely offers numerous benefits, including improved efficiency, cost savings, flexibility, and security. By implementing effective remote configuration management tools and practices, organizations can ensure that their networks remain stable, secure, and scalable, while empowering administrators to manage configurations from anywhere in the world. This shift toward remote management not only simplifies network administration but also enables organizations to adapt to the dynamic needs of modern business environments.

Managing Configuration Files in Multi-Device Environments

In modern networks, especially those that span multiple locations or involve a diverse set of devices, managing configuration files across multiple devices is a significant challenge. As organizations grow and deploy more devices—whether on-premises or in the cloud—the complexity of maintaining consistent configurations increases. Network administrators must ensure that all devices, ranging from routers and switches to firewalls and servers, are correctly configured to work together efficiently and securely. The challenge lies not only in deploying initial configurations but also in managing updates, tracking changes, and ensuring that the network remains operational despite constant adjustments to configurations. Effective management of configuration files in multi-device environments is essential for minimizing errors, ensuring consistency, and maintaining network stability.

One of the first challenges in managing configuration files across multiple devices is the need for consistency. In large networks, administrators are often responsible for configuring hundreds or even thousands of devices. Ensuring that all these devices receive the correct settings is critical to avoid network instability or security vulnerabilities. Configuration management tools such as Ansible, Puppet, and Chef have been developed to address this need by automating the process of configuring multiple devices in a consistent manner. These tools allow administrators to define the desired configuration for each device in a central location and automatically deploy it to all the relevant systems, ensuring that the devices are uniformly configured. This automation reduces the risk of human error and ensures that configurations are applied correctly and consistently across the network.

One of the primary benefits of automated configuration management in multi-device environments is the ability to track changes effectively. As network configurations evolve, administrators need a way to monitor and record changes across the network to maintain oversight and traceability. This is especially important in dynamic environments where configurations are frequently updated to accommodate new devices, features, or security patches. Automated tools provide version control for configuration files, allowing administrators to track who made changes, when they were made, and why. This capability is invaluable when troubleshooting network issues or auditing configurations for security and compliance purposes. By using version control systems integrated with configuration management tools, administrators can easily revert to a previous configuration if something goes wrong, minimizing downtime and preventing operational disruptions.

Managing configuration files in multi-device environments also requires a careful approach to dependencies. Many devices within a network are interconnected and rely on each other to function correctly. For example, a configuration change on a router may affect the behavior of firewalls, servers, or other network appliances that depend on the router for traffic flow. Administrators must ensure that configuration changes do not unintentionally disrupt the operation of other devices. Configuration management tools can help by allowing administrators to define and manage these dependencies, ensuring that configuration changes are applied in the correct order and that all affected devices are properly configured. Additionally, these tools often include testing features that allow administrators to validate configuration changes before they are deployed, helping to identify potential issues before they impact the network.

Another key aspect of managing configuration files in multi-device environments is handling network security. Configuration files often contain sensitive information, such as passwords, access control lists, or encryption keys, which must be protected from unauthorized access. As the number of devices in the network grows, so too does the risk of exposing this sensitive data. Configuration management tools help address this concern by providing secure methods for storing and transferring configuration files. Many tools offer encryption capabilities to protect sensitive data during transit, ensuring that it is not exposed to eavesdropping or tampering. Additionally, some tools provide access control mechanisms that allow administrators to define who can access, modify, and deploy configuration files. This ensures that only authorized personnel can make changes to critical network configurations, reducing the risk of malicious activity.

In multi-device environments, administrators also face the challenge of managing different types of devices and operating systems. A large enterprise network may include a mix of devices running different operating systems or software versions. For example, some devices may be running Linux, while others are running Windows or specialized network operating systems. Configuration management tools must be flexible enough to handle these variations and allow administrators to configure each device according to its specific needs. Many modern configuration management tools are designed to be cross-platform, meaning they can manage devices running a variety of operating systems. These tools use a set of modules or plugins that are tailored to the specific requirements of different operating systems, enabling administrators to apply consistent configuration policies across diverse devices.

The scalability of configuration management is another important consideration in multi-device environments. As networks grow, the number of devices that need to be managed increases, making it essential to have scalable solutions in place. Manual configuration management becomes increasingly impractical as the network expands. Automated configuration management tools allow administrators to scale their operations without adding additional administrative overhead. These tools can handle the configuration of hundreds or thousands of devices, ensuring that all devices are configured consistently and securely, regardless of the size of the network. By integrating configuration management with network monitoring tools, administrators can also gain real-time visibility into the health and performance of devices, allowing them to identify and resolve issues before they escalate.

The challenge of managing configuration files in multi-device environments also extends to compliance and regulatory requirements. Many industries, such as healthcare, finance, and government, have strict regulations that require organizations to maintain certain configuration standards and practices. Network administrators must ensure that configuration files adhere to these standards to avoid fines, legal consequences, or security breaches. Configuration management tools play a vital role in ensuring compliance by automating the application of configuration policies and providing audit trails of all configuration changes. This makes it easier for administrators to demonstrate compliance during audits and respond to any issues that arise related to configuration management.

Furthermore, configuration management systems provide a means for administrators to manage the lifecycle of network configurations. As new devices are added to the network, configuration files need to be updated and deployed to ensure that these devices are correctly configured. When devices are decommissioned or replaced, administrators must ensure that their configurations are securely removed or updated. Lifecycle management features within configuration management tools enable administrators to automate these processes, ensuring that configurations are always up to date and that devices are decommissioned properly. This not only helps to maintain a secure network environment but also ensures that the network infrastructure remains efficient and optimized.

Effective management of configuration files in multi-device environments requires a combination of automation, security, and scalability. Configuration management tools help to address these challenges by providing administrators with the tools they need to deploy, monitor, and maintain configurations across a diverse set of devices. By automating the configuration process, administrators can reduce the risk of human error, improve the consistency of configurations, and ensure that devices are securely configured and maintained. As networks continue to grow and evolve, the importance of managing configuration files efficiently and securely in multi-device environments will only increase, making configuration management a critical component of modern network administration.

The Importance of Backup Protocols in Configuration Management

In the world of network administration, ensuring that configuration files are properly backed up is critical for maintaining network stability and security. Configuration files contain the settings and parameters that define how network devices operate. These settings can range from simple network routing rules to more complex security policies, making them the backbone of a network's functionality. The failure to properly manage and back up these configurations can lead to network downtime, loss of service, and, in the worst-case scenario, irreparable data loss. As a result, backup protocols have become an essential component of configuration management, allowing administrators to safeguard against errors, hardware failures, cyber threats, and unforeseen events.

A backup protocol in configuration management refers to the systematic process of making copies of configuration files and storing them securely, so they can be restored in the event of a failure or disruption. This process ensures that critical configurations are not permanently lost and can be quickly reinstated if necessary. In practice, configuration backups are usually performed on network devices such as routers, switches, firewalls, and servers. Since these devices often contain complex configurations, the ability to revert to a previously backed-up version can save administrators considerable time and effort in restoring network operations.

The role of backup protocols extends beyond simply preventing data loss. They also serve as an essential tool for disaster recovery. In a networked environment, systems can fail for various reasons, including hardware malfunctions, software bugs, power outages, or security breaches. When a failure occurs, a backup configuration ensures that administrators can restore the device to its previous state, minimizing downtime and preventing service interruptions. In large, distributed networks, where multiple devices depend on one another, the absence of backup configurations can lead to cascading failures, amplifying the impact of the initial problem. Backup protocols mitigate this risk by providing a safety net, allowing administrators to restore devices to a known working state without the need for lengthy troubleshooting or reconfiguration.

Backup protocols also play a crucial role in network security. Configuration files can contain sensitive information, such as access control lists, user credentials, and firewall rules, which are critical to safeguarding the network against unauthorized access and cyber threats. If these configurations are lost, overwritten, or corrupted, the network can become vulnerable to attack. Regularly backing up configuration files ensures that administrators have a secure, unaltered copy of the device's configuration, enabling them to quickly restore it to a secure state in the event of a compromise. This is especially important in industries that require compliance with strict regulatory standards, where maintaining the integrity of configuration data is essential for avoiding penalties or security breaches.

One of the key features of backup protocols is the ability to automate the backup process. Manual backups, while necessary, can be error-prone and time-consuming, especially in large networks. By automating backups, administrators can ensure that configuration files are regularly saved without the need for constant intervention. Automation reduces the risk of human error, ensures that backups are consistently performed, and allows administrators to focus on more critical tasks. Tools such as backup schedulers or configuration management systems like Ansible, Chef, and Puppet can automate the backup process, saving time and improving reliability. Automated backup protocols are particularly important in networks with frequent configuration changes, as they allow for the real-time capture of updates, ensuring that the latest configuration is always available for restoration.

The ability to perform incremental backups is another essential aspect of backup protocols. Incremental backups allow only the changes made to the configuration files since the last backup to be stored. This is much more efficient than performing a full backup each time, as it reduces the amount of data that needs to be stored and transferred. Incremental backups ensure that administrators can quickly restore the most recent changes without having to wait for a full backup to complete. For example, if a minor change is made to the configuration of a router, an incremental backup will only store the changes to that configuration, significantly reducing backup time and storage requirements. This is particularly useful in large networks where configuration files can be extensive and frequent backups are necessary.

Backup protocols also help ensure compliance with internal and external standards. Many industries are subject to regulations that require businesses to maintain secure, up-to-date backups of their network configurations. For example, the healthcare industry must comply with the Health Insurance Portability and Accountability Act (HIPAA), which mandates the secure storage of sensitive data, including network configurations. Similarly, the Payment Card Industry Data Security Standard (PCI DSS) requires that organizations maintain secure configurations for systems that process payment information. Backup protocols help organizations comply with these regulations by ensuring that configuration files are stored securely, regularly updated, and available for recovery if needed. In regulated environments, the failure to maintain proper backups can result in costly fines, legal consequences, and reputational damage.

Moreover, backup protocols are invaluable when performing configuration audits. Organizations need to periodically review their network configurations to ensure that they align with security policies, industry standards, and organizational best practices. By maintaining a history of configuration backups, administrators can easily compare current configurations to previous versions, identifying any unauthorized or unintended changes. This historical data is critical for identifying vulnerabilities, preventing configuration drift, and ensuring that network configurations are kept up-to-date and secure. Backup protocols enable administrators to perform these audits efficiently, minimizing the risk of misconfigurations or policy violations.

While backup protocols are essential for protecting configuration data, their effectiveness depends on how and where the backups are stored.

Storing backups locally on the same device or network segment exposes them to the same risks as the primary configuration files, such as data corruption or physical damage to hardware. To mitigate this risk, many organizations opt to store backups in remote locations, such as offsite data centers or cloud storage solutions. Cloud-based backups offer the advantage of geographic redundancy, meaning that even if one location is compromised, the backup remains safe and accessible. Additionally, cloud storage can be highly scalable, allowing organizations to store large volumes of configuration data without worrying about running out of space.

The security of backup files is also a critical consideration. Backup configurations must be encrypted both in transit and at rest to protect them from unauthorized access. Without encryption, backups could be intercepted or stolen, putting sensitive configuration data at risk. Furthermore, access to backup files should be restricted to authorized personnel only. Role-based access control (RBAC) ensures that only those with the appropriate permissions can restore or modify backup files, further securing the backup process.

Backup protocols are an indispensable part of configuration management. They provide network administrators with the tools they need to safeguard, recover, and manage critical configuration files across diverse and dynamic network environments. By automating the backup process, ensuring secure storage, and maintaining an audit trail, backup protocols help protect networks from the risks of misconfigurations, system failures, and security breaches. As networks continue to grow in complexity and importance, maintaining a robust backup strategy will remain a fundamental part of ensuring that network configurations are always protected and recoverable.

Configuration Management Protocols and Compliance Regulations

In today's interconnected world, organizations are required to ensure that their network configurations align with both industry standards and regulatory requirements. Compliance regulations mandate that businesses follow specific guidelines to protect sensitive information, maintain network integrity, and avoid security breaches. These regulations are often stringent and require organizations to document, monitor, and maintain configuration settings to ensure that they are secure and meet the necessary compliance standards. Configuration management protocols are essential tools in meeting these compliance requirements, as they help administrators manage configurations systematically, maintain security, and provide audit trails for regulatory audits. By using these protocols effectively, organizations can mitigate the risks associated with non-compliance, safeguard sensitive data, and ensure that their network environments remain secure.

Compliance regulations, such as the General Data Protection Regulation (GDPR), the Health Insurance Portability and Accountability Act (HIPAA), and the Payment Card Industry Data Security Standard (PCI DSS), place significant importance on the security of data and network infrastructure. These standards require businesses to implement strict controls over how data is stored, processed, and transmitted, as well as how network devices are configured and maintained. Configuration management protocols, such as Secure Copy Protocol (SCP), Simple Network Management Protocol (SNMP), and others, allow administrators to manage network device configurations in a way that adheres to these regulations. By automating and standardizing configuration management, organizations can ensure that their systems are compliant with security policies, reduce the likelihood of human error, and make it easier to enforce configuration standards.

One of the primary roles of configuration management protocols in compliance is to ensure consistency across devices and networks. Regulatory standards often require that specific security settings, such as firewalls, encryption protocols, and user access controls, be applied consistently across all systems in a network. Configuration management protocols help ensure that these settings are uniformly deployed and maintained across all devices. For example, by using automated tools such as Ansible, Puppet, or Chef, administrators can apply configuration files across multiple devices, ensuring that firewalls are configured to meet security policies, encryption standards are applied, and access control lists (ACLs) are consistent throughout the network. This consistency is critical for compliance, as regulatory bodies often require evidence that security controls are enforced across the entire network.

In addition to ensuring consistency, configuration management protocols are essential for providing audit trails. Many compliance regulations mandate that businesses maintain detailed logs of configuration changes, including who made the changes, when they were made, and what was modified. This level of traceability is crucial for demonstrating compliance during audits and for investigating any potential security incidents. Configuration management tools often provide the capability to log all changes to network configurations, creating an audit trail that can be used for compliance verification. For instance, tools like Git, when integrated into network configuration management, can track every modification made to configuration files, providing a clear record of changes over time. This documentation is vital for organizations to prove that they are adhering to regulatory requirements and to identify any potential vulnerabilities that might arise due to unauthorized changes.

Moreover, configuration management protocols help businesses manage the lifecycle of configuration files and network settings. Many regulatory frameworks require that organizations regularly update their systems to address known vulnerabilities, patch security flaws, and apply updates to software and configurations. Configuration management protocols facilitate this by enabling administrators to automate the deployment of configuration updates across devices. By using automated tools to roll out security patches or configuration changes, organizations can ensure that they are complying with the latest security standards without the need for manual intervention. This proactive approach to configuration management reduces the risk of outdated systems and unpatched vulnerabilities, which can leave an organization exposed to regulatory violations or security breaches.

Another critical aspect of configuration management in compliance is the need to maintain secure backups of configuration files. Many regulations require that businesses retain backup copies of their configurations in case of system failure, corruption, or other data loss scenarios. Configuration management protocols help automate the backup process, ensuring that configuration files are securely saved and can be restored in the event of an incident. By regularly backing up configurations and storing them in a secure location, organizations can ensure that they meet compliance requirements for data retention and disaster recovery. These backups also provide a means of recovering from a misconfiguration or malicious attack, allowing administrators to restore systems to their previous secure state.

The role of configuration management protocols in compliance is also closely tied to risk management. Regulatory frameworks often require organizations to assess and mitigate security risks associated with their network infrastructure. By implementing configuration management protocols, administrators can regularly review and update network configurations to align with the latest security best practices and compliance requirements. Configuration management tools can be used to enforce security policies, ensuring that configurations are continually assessed and adjusted as needed to mitigate potential risks. This ability to manage configurations proactively helps organizations stay ahead of emerging threats and regulatory changes, ensuring that their network remains secure and compliant.

The integration of configuration management protocols with monitoring tools further enhances compliance efforts. In many industries, compliance regulations mandate continuous monitoring of network devices to detect any anomalies or unauthorized changes to configurations. By integrating configuration management tools with monitoring platforms, administrators can continuously track the status of devices and configurations, receiving real-time alerts if deviations from established policies are detected. This integration ensures that organizations can quickly respond to potential issues, whether they are the result of configuration drift, unauthorized access, or a security breach, helping to maintain compliance and reduce the likelihood of security incidents.

The complexity of managing configuration files and maintaining compliance across large-scale networks can be overwhelming. However, configuration management protocols, when implemented effectively, provide a streamlined approach to meeting these challenges. Through automation, standardization, and secure backup protocols, these tools allow network administrators to manage configurations consistently and efficiently while ensuring compliance with regulatory requirements. By using these protocols, organizations can reduce the administrative burden of manual configuration management, minimize errors, and improve overall network security. Moreover, the ability to generate audit trails and maintain secure backups ensures that organizations can demonstrate compliance during regulatory audits and quickly recover from any security incidents.

As networks continue to expand and the regulatory landscape becomes more complex, the importance of configuration management in ensuring compliance will only increase. Regulatory requirements are likely to evolve, and organizations will need to adapt to these changes. Configuration management protocols will continue to play a vital role in helping organizations meet these evolving standards, ensuring that their networks are both secure and compliant. By using these protocols as part of a comprehensive security and compliance strategy, administrators can safeguard against risks, streamline compliance efforts, and ensure that network configurations remain aligned with both industry best practices and regulatory mandates.

Real-Time Configuration Management: Applications and Techniques

The complexity of modern networks, systems, and IT infrastructures requires dynamic and agile approaches to configuration management. Real-time configuration management is one such approach, providing administrators with the ability to manage, monitor, and adjust configurations in real-time. Unlike traditional configuration management, which often involves scheduled or batch-based updates, real-time configuration management ensures that systems and devices are consistently optimized, secure, and responsive to changes as they occur. This approach is particularly useful in fast-paced environments where systems need to be updated instantly to maintain network performance, security, and compliance. The applications and techniques of real-time configuration management are wide-ranging, with significant benefits for network reliability, system integrity, and operational efficiency.

In a traditional configuration management setup, updates or changes to system configurations are applied at specified intervals or during maintenance windows. While this works in many environments, it can be inefficient in systems where changes need to be addressed immediately. For example, in network security, if a vulnerability is discovered, it is crucial to apply configuration changes, such as firewall updates or patch deployments, right away to prevent potential attacks. Real-time configuration management enables administrators to make these changes instantly, reducing the time between the identification of an issue and the implementation of a fix. This agility is essential for maintaining a secure and resilient network, particularly in industries that face constant threats and need to respond to them rapidly.

One of the key applications of real-time configuration management is in the realm of network security. In an environment where cyber threats are constantly evolving, systems must be configured to adapt and respond to new vulnerabilities quickly. Real-time configuration management enables administrators to implement security patches, reconfigure firewalls, adjust access control lists, or even shut down compromised systems on the fly. This dynamic approach helps mitigate the risks associated with cyberattacks, such as ransomware, DDoS attacks, or unauthorized access, by ensuring that security measures are always up to date. Moreover, real-time configuration management allows for continuous monitoring of network devices, so administrators can detect suspicious behavior, reconfigure settings, and take preventive measures before security breaches can occur.

Beyond security, real-time configuration management is also critical for maintaining system performance. For example, in environments that handle large amounts of data, such as cloud computing platforms or high-traffic websites, real-time adjustments to system configurations can prevent bottlenecks or downtime. In such environments, automatic scaling of resources—such as adding more storage, adjusting processing power, or reconfiguring load balancers—can be crucial for maintaining optimal performance. Real-time configuration management allows these adjustments to be made instantly based on traffic patterns or system load, ensuring that the infrastructure adapts to demand without manual intervention. This ability to adjust system parameters in real-time also supports high availability and fault tolerance, which are critical for organizations that rely on 24/7 uptime.

In large, distributed systems, such as data centers or multi-cloud environments, real-time configuration management helps maintain uniformity across various devices and services. The complexity of these systems means that manual updates can lead to inconsistencies or configuration drift, where different devices or servers may have different settings, potentially causing performance degradation or failures. Real-time management ensures that configuration changes are propagated across the network or cloud services instantly, keeping all devices synchronized and aligned with the desired configuration state. This is particularly important in environments that rely on automation and orchestration tools, where real-time updates to configurations can support a seamless, integrated workflow across multiple platforms and systems.

One of the key techniques for real-time configuration management involves the use of automation and orchestration tools. Tools like Ansible, Puppet, Chef, and SaltStack are commonly used to manage configurations in real-time. These tools allow administrators to define configuration files or playbooks that describe the desired state of a system or network. When a change is required—whether it's a software update, security patch, or a configuration tweak—the tool automatically applies the necessary changes across all affected devices or systems. This automation can be triggered in response to events such as system alerts, threshold crossings, or manually issued commands. The key advantage of this technique is that it eliminates the need for human intervention, ensuring that systems are configured according to predefined standards while also allowing for immediate adjustments when necessary.

The integration of real-time configuration management with monitoring systems further enhances its capabilities. By combining configuration management with real-time monitoring tools, administrators can not only apply configuration changes instantly but also receive continuous feedback on system performance. Monitoring tools can track metrics such as CPU usage, memory utilization, network traffic, and error rates, triggering real-time configuration adjustments when certain thresholds are reached. For example, if a server begins to experience high load, the monitoring system can trigger a real-time configuration change to scale up resources or offload traffic to other servers. This integrated approach creates a responsive, self-healing system where configuration changes are applied automatically based on real-time data, reducing the need for manual intervention and enhancing system reliability.

Another essential technique in real-time configuration management is the use of version control and rollback mechanisms. While real-time changes are beneficial for immediate adjustments, they also introduce the risk of making errors or introducing instability into a system. To mitigate this risk, configuration management systems often incorporate version control features that track every configuration change and maintain a history of configurations. In the event that a configuration change causes problems, administrators can quickly roll back to a previous, known-good version of the configuration. This technique ensures that the system remains stable and that administrators can recover from misconfigurations without significant downtime. The ability to revert changes quickly is particularly important in environments where uptime is critical, and real-time management needs to be balanced with caution.

Real-time configuration management also plays a vital role in compliance and regulatory adherence. Many industries, such as healthcare, finance, and government, are subject to strict regulations regarding data protection, network security, and system integrity. These regulations often require businesses to implement specific configurations for devices and systems and to monitor and record configuration changes for auditing purposes. Real-time configuration management tools enable organizations to ensure that systems are always compliant with these standards by allowing immediate application of necessary configuration updates. Furthermore, they enable organizations to maintain accurate logs of all configuration changes, which are essential for audit trails and compliance reporting.

The scalability of real-time configuration management is another significant benefit for modern network environments. As networks and systems expand, the need to manage configurations across a growing number of devices becomes increasingly complex. Real-time configuration management systems are designed to handle large-scale environments efficiently, enabling administrators to apply changes across thousands of devices simultaneously. This scalability ensures that as businesses grow, their network infrastructure can scale seamlessly while maintaining consistent and optimized configurations.

Real-time configuration management is an indispensable tool for maintaining the security, performance, and compliance of modern IT infrastructures. The ability to apply immediate configuration changes ensures that systems can adapt to dynamic environments, respond to security threats, and maintain operational efficiency. Techniques such as automation, orchestration, version control, and integration with monitoring systems provide administrators with the tools they need to manage configurations proactively and in real-time. As networks become more complex and demands for agility and responsiveness increase, real-time configuration management will continue to be a vital component in ensuring the smooth operation of modern IT systems.

Using Configuration Management Protocols for System Updates and Patches

In the fast-paced world of network administration, keeping systems up to date is a critical task to ensure security, stability, and performance. Whether it's patching software vulnerabilities, applying security fixes, or updating configurations to support new features, timely and accurate updates are essential to maintaining a healthy IT infrastructure. Configuration management protocols provide a powerful framework for automating and streamlining the process of managing system updates and patches across diverse systems, devices, and environments. By leveraging these protocols, network administrators can reduce the risk of human error, improve efficiency, and ensure that updates are applied consistently and securely.

System updates and patches are essential for maintaining the security and functionality of software applications, operating systems, and network devices. As vulnerabilities are discovered or new features are released, manufacturers and developers frequently release updates and patches to address these issues. If these updates are not applied in a timely manner, systems become increasingly vulnerable to security breaches, performance degradation, and even system failures. Configuration management protocols, such as Secure Copy Protocol (SCP), Trivial File Transfer Protocol (TFTP), Simple Network Management Protocol (SNMP), and others, provide the tools necessary to deploy updates and patches efficiently and securely across large-scale, complex environments.

One of the primary advantages of using configuration management protocols for system updates is automation. Manual updates can be time-consuming, error-prone, and inconsistent, especially in large networks with hundreds or thousands of devices. By automating the update process, administrators can ensure that updates are applied quickly and uniformly across all systems, reducing the risk of missed updates or configuration errors. Automated tools such as Ansible, Puppet, Chef, and SaltStack integrate with configuration management protocols to deploy updates and patches across devices in real-time, ensuring that all systems are kept up to date with the latest security fixes and configuration changes. These tools allow administrators to define configuration policies, specify the desired state of devices, and automatically push updates to the entire network without needing to manually intervene on each device.

Automating the update process not only improves efficiency but also ensures consistency. In multi-device environments, keeping configurations consistent across devices is crucial for network stability and security. When administrators rely on manual updates, it is easy for some devices to fall behind on updates or patches, resulting in inconsistencies that can lead to network disruptions or security vulnerabilities. By using configuration management protocols, administrators can ensure that updates are applied in a standardized manner, regardless of the type of device, operating system, or application being used. This consistency is vital for maintaining a secure, reliable network infrastructure, especially in large or complex environments where manual updates would be too time-consuming and prone to errors.

Security is a central concern when applying system updates and patches, and configuration management protocols play a critical role in ensuring that updates are deployed securely. Many updates and patches contain important security fixes that protect systems from cyber threats, such as malware, ransomware, and other types of attacks. If these updates are not applied securely, they can potentially expose systems to the very vulnerabilities they were designed to mitigate. Configuration management tools that leverage secure file transfer protocols, such as SCP or SFTP, ensure that updates are transferred between systems securely, with encryption and authentication mechanisms that protect data during transmission. These protocols prevent unauthorized access or tampering during the update process, ensuring that patches and configuration updates are applied securely without risking the integrity of the system.

Another important feature of configuration management protocols is the ability to manage dependencies and versioning. Many system updates and patches are interdependent, meaning that one update may require other updates or configurations to be applied beforehand. Without careful management, it can be difficult to track which updates need to be applied first and which systems need specific versions of software. Configuration management tools help administrators track these dependencies and manage the sequencing of updates to ensure that all necessary patches are applied in the correct order. Version control features built into configuration management protocols also allow administrators to roll back to previous versions of configurations if an update causes unforeseen issues, providing a fail-safe mechanism to recover from problems introduced by new patches or updates.

The use of configuration management protocols also provides a centralized approach to system updates, making it easier for administrators to monitor and track the status of updates across an entire network. In large organizations, especially those with distributed systems, keeping track of which devices have received which updates can be a challenge. By using configuration management tools, administrators can maintain a centralized repository of configuration files and updates, ensuring that all devices are updated according to the same schedule and policy. This centralization simplifies reporting and auditing, as administrators can quickly check the status of updates across devices and identify any systems that have failed to apply the latest patches. Additionally, many configuration management tools include reporting features that allow administrators to generate detailed logs of updates and changes, making it easier to track compliance with organizational policies or regulatory requirements.

In highly regulated industries, such as finance, healthcare, and government, compliance with security and privacy regulations is essential. These industries often require organizations to maintain up-to-date systems and apply security patches promptly to protect sensitive data. Configuration management protocols help ensure compliance by automating the application of patches and updates, allowing organizations to demonstrate that they are meeting industry standards for security and data protection. Moreover, the audit trails generated by configuration management tools provide detailed records of when updates were applied, who approved them, and what changes were made, enabling organizations to meet compliance requirements and provide evidence during audits.

Real-time monitoring and feedback are also key components of modern configuration management protocols. By integrating configuration management tools with network monitoring systems, administrators can receive immediate feedback on the success or failure of updates. This real-time monitoring ensures that if an update causes issues or conflicts, administrators can take corrective action quickly, minimizing downtime and disruptions. For example, if an update causes a service to fail or a system to crash, the monitoring system can trigger an alert, and the administrator can use the configuration management tool to roll back the change or apply a fix. This proactive approach helps maintain network stability and ensures that updates do not compromise the overall functionality of the system.

The flexibility of configuration management protocols makes them suitable for a wide range of network environments, from small businesses to large enterprises. These protocols can be used in traditional on-premises networks, hybrid cloud environments, and fully cloud-based infrastructures, ensuring that updates are applied consistently and securely across all types of systems. As organizations continue to embrace cloud computing and virtualization, the ability to manage updates and patches across a mix of physical and virtual environments becomes increasingly important. Configuration management protocols provide the scalability and flexibility needed to meet these challenges, ensuring that updates are applied seamlessly across diverse infrastructure.

The role of configuration management protocols in system updates and patches cannot be overstated. They provide the automation, security, and consistency required to maintain up-to-date systems while minimizing the risk of errors and downtime. By automating the update process, managing dependencies, and securing file transfers, these protocols help ensure that networks remain secure, stable, and compliant with regulatory requirements. Whether applied to traditional networks or modern cloud environments, configuration management protocols play a critical role in the ongoing maintenance and security of IT infrastructures.

Best Practices for Configuration File Integrity and Verification

In any network or IT infrastructure, configuration files are the cornerstone of operational stability. These files dictate how devices, applications, and systems interact, and they often contain critical settings, from network security policies to operational parameters. The integrity of these configuration files is essential, as even a small error or unauthorized modification can lead to network vulnerabilities, service disruptions, or compliance violations. Therefore, ensuring the integrity and verification of configuration files is a critical practice for network administrators and IT professionals. Establishing and following best practices for configuration file integrity and verification helps maintain system security, prevent errors, and ensure that changes align with organizational policies and regulatory requirements.

One of the first and most important practices for maintaining configuration file integrity is the use of version control. As configuration files are updated, having a version-controlled system allows administrators to track changes, roll back to previous versions, and ensure that only approved modifications are made. Version control systems such as Git, Subversion, or Mercurial are commonly used to manage configuration files, providing a comprehensive history of changes. This allows administrators to see who made the change, what was changed, and why the modification was necessary. Version control not only ensures that configuration changes can be tracked and audited but also provides a mechanism to revert to known stable versions if a recent change causes problems. This method is particularly beneficial in environments where configuration changes are frequent, and multiple administrators may be involved in making modifications.

Another essential practice for configuration file integrity is implementing strict access controls. Only authorized personnel should have the ability to modify configuration files, as unauthorized changes can introduce security risks, errors, or even sabotage. Role-based access control (RBAC) and the principle of least privilege should be enforced to ensure that only those who need access to specific configuration files can modify them. Administrators should also establish clear policies for who can approve, review, and implement configuration changes. By limiting access to configuration files, organizations can reduce the risk of accidental or malicious modifications. Additionally, integrating access control with auditing systems ensures that any changes to configuration files are logged, providing a clear trail for security monitoring and compliance audits.

Regular backup and secure storage of configuration files is another critical best practice. Even with strict access controls and versioning in place, unforeseen issues such as data corruption, hardware failure, or malicious attacks can compromise configuration files. Maintaining regular backups ensures that a secure copy of configuration files is always available for recovery. These backups should be stored in secure locations, such as offsite data centers or encrypted cloud storage, to prevent unauthorized access. Additionally, backups should be encrypted both at rest and in transit to protect sensitive data. Automating the backup process, along with regular testing of backup integrity, helps ensure that the backup files are up-to-date and can be restored promptly if necessary.

One of the most effective methods for verifying the integrity of configuration files is the use of checksum or hash algorithms.

Checksums and hashes are cryptographic representations of files that can be used to verify their integrity. By calculating the checksum or hash value of a configuration file at a specific point in time and comparing it with the current value, administrators can determine if the file has been altered. This technique helps detect unauthorized changes or corruption of configuration files. Administrators should periodically calculate and compare checksums or hashes for critical configuration files, particularly after updates or changes, to ensure that the files remain intact. For enhanced security, administrators can use trusted third-party services or centralized systems to store and compare hashes, further reducing the risk of tampering.

Automating configuration verification is also an effective practice for ensuring integrity. Automated tools can be used to compare configuration files against predefined templates or best practices to detect discrepancies. These tools can help ensure that configuration files adhere to security policies, organizational standards, and compliance regulations. Automated configuration verification tools can run continuous checks to identify issues such as unauthorized changes, missing security settings, or non-compliance with configuration baselines. By integrating automated verification into the configuration management process, organizations can quickly detect and address configuration issues before they impact operations or security.

To further enhance configuration integrity, it is important to implement change management processes that include rigorous testing and validation procedures. Before configuration changes are applied to live environments, they should undergo thorough testing to ensure they perform as expected and do not introduce errors or security vulnerabilities. In test environments that mimic production systems, configuration changes should be reviewed and tested in isolation to verify that they will not cause any unintended consequences. This practice helps ensure that new configurations are stable, secure, and functional before they are deployed across the network. After deployment, the changes should be continuously monitored for performance and security to identify any potential issues early.

Configuration file integrity can also be protected by using encryption for sensitive data stored within these files. Configuration files may contain sensitive information such as passwords, access keys, or encryption keys, which must be kept secure. If this information is not properly encrypted, it can be exposed during unauthorized access or when configuration files are transferred over unsecured networks. Administrators should use encryption to protect sensitive data within configuration files, ensuring that only authorized users or systems can decrypt and access this information. Additionally, encryption should be applied during configuration file transfers to protect data from interception during transmission.

Another important practice for maintaining configuration file integrity is establishing a robust auditing and monitoring system. Continuous monitoring allows administrators to track real-time changes to configuration files and detect any anomalies or unauthorized activities. By integrating auditing systems with version control and access controls, organizations can create a comprehensive audit trail that provides visibility into who made changes, when they were made, and the reasons behind them. This trail is invaluable for detecting potential security incidents, addressing compliance violations, and understanding the impact of changes. Automated alerts can notify administrators immediately if configuration files are altered outside of approved processes, allowing for quick responses to unauthorized activities.

Finally, integrating configuration management practices with network monitoring and security tools helps maintain ongoing configuration integrity. By continuously monitoring network devices and configurations, organizations can detect any configuration drift, which occurs when a device's configuration deviates from its intended state over time. Configuration drift can result from unapproved changes, misconfigurations, or the accumulation of minor adjustments that lead to significant issues. Tools that integrate configuration management with network monitoring can automatically alert administrators to drift, enabling them to quickly correct the configuration and bring the device back into compliance with network standards.

Maintaining the integrity of configuration files is a fundamental aspect of network and system management. By adopting best practices such as version control, access control, encryption, automated verification, and rigorous testing, organizations can ensure that their configuration files remain secure, consistent, and reliable. The use of comprehensive auditing and monitoring tools, along with effective change management processes, further enhances the ability to maintain configuration integrity, allowing administrators to manage configurations proactively and securely. As network environments continue to grow and evolve, these best practices will continue to be vital in ensuring that configurations remain intact and functional, minimizing risks and supporting operational efficiency.

Customizing Configuration Management Protocols for Specific Network Requirements

In the rapidly evolving world of network management, one-size-fits-all solutions are seldom sufficient. As networks become more complex and diverse, the need to tailor configuration management protocols to specific network requirements has grown significantly. Configuration management protocols are essential tools for ensuring that network devices are properly configured, updated, and maintained. However, different network environments have varying needs depending on the size, scope, and complexity of the infrastructure, as well as specific performance, security, and compliance requirements. Customizing configuration management protocols to address these specific needs is vital for ensuring optimal network performance, security, and scalability. This approach involves adapting protocols to meet the unique demands of the organization's network while maintaining the benefits of automation, consistency, and security.

Customizing configuration management protocols often starts with a clear understanding of the network's structure and the types of devices involved. In large-scale networks, for example, managing configurations across hundreds or thousands of devices, such as routers, switches, firewalls, and servers, requires a high degree of automation and control. For these types of environments, administrators may choose to use protocols such as Ansible, Puppet, or Chef, which can be customized to handle a diverse set of devices and configurations. These protocols allow for the creation of modular configuration templates and scripts that can be easily adapted to different devices, operating systems, or environments, streamlining the process of configuration management.

One of the key areas where customization plays a significant role is in automating configuration deployments across heterogeneous environments. Different network devices often run on different operating systems or have unique configuration requirements. For instance, a network router running Cisco IOS may have different configuration parameters than a Linux-based server or a cloud service instance. By customizing configuration management protocols, administrators can create device-specific modules or scripts that ensure each device is configured correctly according to its own set of requirements. For instance, a network administrator might use customized Ansible playbooks that adjust the configuration of a Cisco device, apply specific firewall rules on a Linux server, and provision cloud instances based on templates that meet organizational standards. The flexibility of modern configuration management protocols enables administrators to fine-tune their deployment strategies to ensure that each device receives the correct settings in a consistent and automated manner.

Another key aspect of customization involves security requirements. Security is a top priority in any network, and each organization has its own set of security policies and regulatory compliance requirements that must be adhered to. Customizing configuration management protocols to enforce these security policies ensures that all devices and configurations comply with the organization's security standards. For example, some networks may require strict encryption standards, such as enforcing the use of specific SSL/TLS versions or enforcing strong password policies across all devices. Configuration management tools like Chef or Puppet can be customized to include these security requirements in configuration templates or scripts, ensuring that all devices are automatically configured to comply with the organization's security posture. In environments subject to regulatory compliance, such as healthcare or finance, these tools can help enforce policies that align with industry regulations like HIPAA or PCI DSS, making it easier to demonstrate compliance during audits.

Performance optimization is another area where customizing configuration management protocols is crucial. Networks often have specific performance needs that must be met to ensure optimal operation. For instance, an enterprise network might need to prioritize the performance of critical applications, while ensuring that other systems, such as testing or development environments, do not impact the overall network performance. Customization of configuration management protocols allows administrators to tailor configurations based on these needs. For example, custom templates can be developed to apply Quality of Service (QoS) settings that prioritize certain types of traffic over others, or to configure network devices to balance load effectively across multiple servers. By fine-tuning these settings, network administrators can ensure that the network meets performance requirements, reduces congestion, and optimizes traffic flow.

In large-scale or geographically distributed networks, the ability to customize configuration management protocols for specific locations or network segments becomes particularly important. Multi-site environments, for instance, require careful coordination to ensure that configuration changes are applied consistently across all locations. Customization allows administrators to segment configuration management tasks based on location or role. For example, different branches of a company may have unique network requirements based on local traffic patterns or regional regulations. By customizing configuration management protocols to handle site-specific configurations, administrators can ensure that the right settings are applied at each location, while still maintaining centralized control. This approach enables network administrators to manage large, distributed networks efficiently, ensuring that all devices are configured according to their specific needs without sacrificing consistency or control.

Scalability is another factor that requires customization of configuration management protocols. As organizations grow and their network infrastructures expand, it becomes necessary to adapt configuration management protocols to accommodate new devices, applications, and network segments. Customization ensures that the protocol is flexible enough to scale with the growing network, enabling administrators to add new devices or systems without disrupting existing configurations. For example, a cloud-based network may rapidly scale as additional virtual machines or services are provisioned. By customizing configuration management protocols to handle the dynamic nature of cloud environments, administrators can automate the configuration of new instances and integrate them seamlessly into the existing network. This ability to scale configurations ensures that the network remains manageable and secure as the organization grows.

Furthermore, customizing configuration management protocols can also improve the ease of integration with other network management tools. For example, network monitoring, logging, and incident response tools may need to be integrated with the configuration management process to provide a comprehensive view of network health and performance. Customization of configuration management protocols can ensure that configuration changes trigger appropriate monitoring or logging events, enabling real-time feedback on network status. This integration enhances the ability to detect and respond to issues quickly, improving overall network reliability and security.

While customizing configuration management protocols offers numerous advantages, it also requires careful planning and attention to detail. One of the challenges of customization is maintaining a balance between flexibility and complexity. Over-customization can lead to overly complicated systems that are difficult to manage, while insufficient customization may fail to meet the specific needs of the network. Administrators must ensure that the customizations they implement are well-documented, maintainable, and scalable, and that they do not introduce unnecessary complexity into the management process. Additionally, regular testing and validation of customized protocols are essential to ensure that they continue to meet network requirements as the environment evolves.

Customizing configuration management protocols for specific network requirements is a vital practice for modern network administrators. Whether optimizing security, improving performance, ensuring regulatory compliance, or managing large-scale networks, customization enables administrators to tailor configuration management tools to meet their unique needs. By carefully designing and implementing customized configuration management protocols, organizations can maintain a flexible, scalable, and secure network environment that adapts to their changing needs.

Integrating TFTP with SNMP for Network Device Configuration

In modern network management, configuring and maintaining network devices efficiently is a crucial task for administrators. Ensuring that devices such as routers, switches, firewalls, and other network appliances are properly configured and up-to-date is essential for network stability, security, and performance. While several protocols exist for managing configurations, two particularly useful protocols are Trivial File Transfer Protocol (TFTP) and Simple Network Management Protocol (SNMP). TFTP is widely used for transferring configuration files and system images between network devices, while SNMP is an essential tool for monitoring and managing network devices. Integrating TFTP with SNMP can create a robust system for automating the configuration of network devices, improving efficiency and enabling more proactive management.

TFTP is a lightweight file transfer protocol that allows for the quick transfer of files between devices over a network. Unlike FTP or SFTP, TFTP does not provide encryption or security features, but its simplicity makes it an attractive choice for environments where security is not a major concern, and speed and low overhead are paramount. TFTP is commonly used for booting network devices, transferring system images, and deploying configuration files to devices that support it. For instance, many network devices, such as switches and routers, use TFTP to retrieve their configuration files from a centralized server upon startup. The ability to push configuration files to multiple devices quickly and automatically is a significant advantage of using TFTP in network device management.

However, while TFTP is excellent for file transfers, it lacks the monitoring and management capabilities necessary for a comprehensive network management solution. This is where SNMP comes in. SNMP is a protocol designed for monitoring and managing network devices. It allows network administrators to remotely monitor the health and status of devices, retrieve performance metrics, and make configuration changes. SNMP uses a client-server architecture, with network devices running SNMP agents that report data to a central management system. The protocol allows administrators to query devices for status information, modify configuration settings, and receive alerts or traps in response to significant events. SNMP is particularly useful for keeping track of device performance, detecting issues early, and managing large-scale networks.

The integration of TFTP with SNMP provides a powerful combination that streamlines network configuration management. By combining TFTP's ability to quickly transfer configuration files with SNMP's robust monitoring and management capabilities, administrators can automate the process of configuration deployment, monitor the status of network devices in real-time, and ensure that devices are always operating with the correct configurations. For example, an administrator can use SNMP to monitor a network device and detect when a configuration change or update is needed, then automatically use TFTP to push the new configuration to the device without manual intervention.

One key advantage of integrating TFTP with SNMP is the ability to automate network configuration changes based on device status. With SNMP, administrators can collect real-time data on device performance, such as CPU usage, memory usage, interface status, and network traffic. If an SNMP agent detects a problem or anomaly, such as a router interface being down or memory usage reaching critical levels, it can trigger a TFTP-based configuration update to restore the device to its desired state. For example, if a router's configuration is incorrect or if there is a need to apply a security patch, SNMP can initiate a TFTP request to transfer the correct configuration file to the device, ensuring that it is restored to the proper state.

Another critical benefit of integrating TFTP and SNMP is the ability to streamline bulk configuration changes across large networks. In large, distributed networks, manually updating the configuration of each device can be a daunting and error-prone task. By using SNMP to monitor device health and configuration status and TFTP to transfer the necessary configuration files, administrators can automate the process of applying updates or changes across multiple devices simultaneously. This integration ensures consistency across all devices in the network and minimizes the risk of human error, which can often result in misconfigurations or overlooked devices. For example, if a network-wide firmware update is required, SNMP can be used to query all devices to ensure they are running the correct version, and TFTP can be used to deploy the new firmware to all devices quickly and reliably.

The integration of TFTP and SNMP also enhances network security. Many network devices require periodic configuration updates or patches to address security vulnerabilities. Traditionally, this task would involve manually uploading configuration files to each device, which is not only time-consuming but also leaves room for error. By automating the process using SNMP and TFTP, administrators can ensure that security patches are applied consistently and promptly across the entire network. Furthermore, the SNMP protocol allows administrators to monitor for unauthorized changes to configurations. If a device's configuration deviates from the desired state, SNMP can alert administrators, allowing them to respond quickly and use TFTP to push the correct configuration file to the device.

Moreover, SNMP traps can be set up to trigger specific actions when critical thresholds are reached. For example, if a device experiences a significant network performance degradation or goes offline, an SNMP trap could alert the administrator to investigate. As part of the response, the system can automatically invoke TFTP to reload or restore a known good configuration to the device. This proactive approach allows for quick resolution of network issues, reducing downtime and preventing potential network failures from escalating into larger problems.

The combination of TFTP and SNMP is particularly beneficial for managing configurations in cloud-based or hybrid environments. These types of networks often consist of a mix of physical and virtual devices, requiring constant configuration management across diverse platforms. With TFTP's ability to deliver configuration files quickly and SNMP's ability to monitor and manage devices in real-time, administrators can seamlessly manage both physical and virtual devices, ensuring that each device is always operating with the correct settings. This integration is also valuable in environments where devices are constantly being provisioned or decommissioned, as it allows administrators to automate the configuration of new devices and apply the appropriate settings based on real-time monitoring.

However, integrating TFTP with SNMP also presents certain challenges. One of the primary concerns is the security of the data being transferred, particularly since TFTP does not inherently include encryption or authentication mechanisms. To mitigate this risk, administrators should consider using SNMPv3, which offers stronger security features such as encryption and authentication. Additionally, administrators can implement network security measures such as VPNs, firewalls, and access control lists to protect the communication channels between devices and the central management system. This ensures that even though TFTP is used to transfer configuration files, the overall system remains secure from potential threats.

In conclusion, integrating TFTP with SNMP provides network administrators with a powerful toolset for managing device configurations, improving efficiency, and ensuring that devices remain up-to-date and secure. The ability to monitor devices in real-time and apply configuration changes instantly reduces the risk of misconfigurations and security vulnerabilities, while automation simplifies the management of large, complex networks. Whether applied to traditional on-premises networks or modern cloud-based environments, the combination of TFTP and SNMP enables administrators to maintain network stability, optimize performance, and ensure that configurations are always aligned with organizational and security requirements. This integration is a cornerstone of modern network management, offering both flexibility and reliability in the face of growing network demands.

The Role of Cloud-Based Configuration Management Tools

The rapid growth of cloud computing and the increasing reliance on cloud-based infrastructures have transformed the way organizations approach network and system management. In particular, cloud-based configuration management tools have become essential for managing configurations across distributed, scalable, and often hybrid network environments. These tools provide administrators with the ability to automate, monitor, and enforce configuration policies across vast networks of virtual and physical devices. As the complexity of modern IT infrastructures continues to grow, the role of cloud-based configuration management tools has become even more crucial in ensuring that systems are configured correctly, securely, and consistently.

One of the key advantages of cloud-based configuration management tools is their ability to simplify the management of complex, multi-cloud, and hybrid environments. In traditional on-premises environments, administrators had to manually configure each device and system, often requiring significant time and resources. Cloud-based tools, however, allow administrators to manage configurations centrally, regardless of whether the devices are on-premises, in a private cloud, or across multiple public cloud platforms. These tools integrate with cloud services such as Amazon Web Services (AWS), Microsoft Azure, or Google Cloud Platform (GCP), enabling administrators to automate the configuration and management of resources in real-time. This integration reduces the complexity of managing multiple environments and ensures that configurations are applied consistently across all systems, whether they are virtual machines, containers, or on-premises servers.

Cloud-based configuration management tools are particularly effective in handling the scalability demands of modern organizations. With the rapid provisioning and decommissioning of virtual machines and other cloud resources, it can be challenging to ensure that all devices are configured correctly. Cloud-based tools address this challenge by enabling administrators to define configuration policies that can be automatically applied to new resources as they are spun up in the cloud. For example, when a new virtual machine is launched in AWS or Azure, the configuration management tool can automatically apply the necessary security settings, network configurations, and software installations based on predefined templates or policies. This automation ensures that each new resource is configured according to organizational standards without requiring manual intervention, making it possible to scale infrastructure quickly while maintaining consistent configurations.

The use of cloud-based configuration management tools also enhances agility and flexibility in modern network environments. Organizations today need to respond quickly to changing business needs, customer demands, or security threats. Cloud-based tools allow administrators to make configuration changes across the entire infrastructure in minutes, rather than hours or days. This speed is particularly beneficial when dealing with time-sensitive issues, such as applying security patches or addressing performance bottlenecks. Cloud-based configuration management tools often provide features that allow for real-time updates, ensuring that the entire network is consistently aligned with the latest configurations. This ability to rapidly adapt to changes enables organizations to maintain optimal network performance and security while avoiding prolonged downtime or service disruptions.

Security is one of the most critical aspects of modern network and system management, and cloud-based configuration management tools play an integral role in ensuring that devices are configured securely. Many of the security issues organizations face today stem from misconfigurations, such as exposed ports, weak access controls, or outdated software versions. Cloud-based configuration management tools enable administrators to enforce security policies across the entire infrastructure, ensuring that security settings are consistently applied to all devices. For example, administrators can define policies that mandate the use of encryption protocols, multi-factor authentication, and proper firewall configurations, and the tool will automatically apply these settings to all cloud resources. By automating security configuration, organizations can reduce the risk of vulnerabilities caused by human error or inconsistent configurations, significantly enhancing their overall security posture.

In addition to security, cloud-based configuration management tools help organizations achieve regulatory compliance. Many industries, such as healthcare, finance, and telecommunications, are subject to strict regulatory requirements that mandate the use of specific security measures and configuration standards. Cloud-based tools allow administrators to automate compliance checks by defining configuration templates that meet the requirements of various regulatory frameworks, such as HIPAA, PCI-DSS, or GDPR. These tools can continuously monitor configurations and alert administrators to any deviations from compliance standards. In the event of an audit, the tool can generate reports that provide evidence of compliance, simplifying the audit process and helping organizations avoid fines or penalties.

Furthermore, cloud-based configuration management tools enable organizations to manage infrastructure as code (IaC), a practice that allows network and system configurations to be defined, versioned, and managed in code form. This approach provides a number of benefits, including the ability to track changes, roll back configurations, and automate deployments. IaC tools such as Terraform, AWS CloudFormation, or Azure Resource Manager can be integrated with cloud-based configuration management tools to ensure that all resources are configured according to best practices. This integration allows administrators to define infrastructure requirements in a declarative manner, ensuring that the desired state of the infrastructure is maintained at all times. IaC also makes it easier to replicate configurations across different environments, improving consistency and reducing the risk of configuration drift.

The ability to monitor and audit configurations is another key benefit of cloud-based configuration management tools. Many of these tools provide built-in monitoring capabilities that allow administrators to track the status of configurations in real-time. This continuous monitoring enables organizations to identify configuration drift—when a system deviates from its intended configuration—before it becomes a significant issue. Additionally, cloud-based tools can generate detailed audit logs that record every configuration change, including who made the change, when it was made, and what was altered. These logs are invaluable for troubleshooting, security investigations, and compliance audits. By providing visibility into configuration changes, cloud-based tools help ensure that administrators can quickly identify and address issues as they arise, reducing the risk of downtime or security incidents.

As organizations continue to adopt hybrid and multi-cloud environments, the need for centralized configuration management has become even more important. Cloud-based configuration management tools enable organizations to manage configurations across multiple cloud platforms, on-premises systems, and hybrid infrastructures from a single interface. This centralized approach simplifies the management of diverse environments, reduces the risk of inconsistencies, and improves operational efficiency. Whether an organization is running a mix of virtual machines, containers, or serverless architectures, cloud-based configuration management tools can adapt to the unique requirements of each platform, providing a unified view of the entire infrastructure.

Cloud-based configuration management tools also promote collaboration and standardization within teams. By using centralized, version-controlled templates and configuration policies, teams can collaborate more effectively, ensuring that configurations align with organizational best practices. These tools provide a single source of truth for configuration standards, making it easier for administrators to manage complex systems and avoid configuration errors. Collaboration features, such as shared templates, version control, and automated deployment pipelines, allow teams to work together seamlessly, reducing the likelihood of miscommunication and improving the overall efficiency of the configuration management process.

The role of cloud-based configuration management tools continues to evolve as organizations adopt more advanced technologies such as containers, microservices, and serverless computing. These tools are designed to handle the unique challenges posed by these technologies, ensuring that configurations are applied consistently and securely across dynamic, distributed environments. With the increasing complexity of IT infrastructures, the importance of cloud-based configuration management tools cannot be overstated. These tools provide the automation, flexibility, security, and scalability that organizations need to manage their network and system configurations effectively, making them a critical component of modern IT operations.

Automation and Orchestration in Configuration Management

In the rapidly evolving landscape of IT infrastructure, automation and orchestration have become integral components of configuration management. As organizations scale their systems, manage increasing complexity, and strive for efficiency, these tools offer a powerful means to streamline processes and ensure that network devices and services are configured consistently, securely, and optimally. While configuration management provides the framework for defining and applying the desired state of infrastructure, automation and orchestration serve as the mechanisms that make this process faster, more reliable, and more efficient. By leveraging automation and orchestration, businesses can achieve a higher level of control and reduce the risks associated with manual intervention, such as human error and inconsistency.

At the heart of configuration management is the idea of ensuring that devices, services, and systems are set up and maintained in a consistent and predictable manner. Automation and orchestration build upon this concept by adding the capability to automate the deployment, configuration, and management of systems across large-scale environments. With the increasing demand for rapid deployment of systems and services, traditional manual processes have become inadequate to keep pace. Instead, automation tools such as Ansible, Puppet, Chef, and SaltStack have emerged as crucial enablers of efficiency in configuration management. These tools allow administrators to write scripts, templates, or playbooks that define the desired configurations of systems and applications, which are then automatically applied across devices, services, and environments.

The role of automation in configuration management goes far beyond simple scripting or one-time configuration updates. By automating repetitive tasks, configuration management tools reduce the amount of manual labor required for system provisioning, patch management, and software deployment. For instance, in a network environment, automation can be used to apply the same configuration file to multiple devices at once, ensuring that all systems are consistently configured. Furthermore, automation can help enforce policies and standards across the entire network, ensuring compliance and reducing the chances of errors or misconfigurations. This consistent and automated approach minimizes the risk of security vulnerabilities, performance issues, and configuration drift, where devices become misaligned with the desired configuration over time.

Orchestration, on the other hand, adds an additional layer of complexity by enabling the coordination and integration of multiple automation processes. While automation focuses on individual tasks, orchestration coordinates a series of tasks or workflows, allowing for the management of multiple systems and devices simultaneously. Orchestration tools like Kubernetes, Apache Airflow, or Terraform work by managing interdependent services and ensuring that tasks are completed in the correct order. For example, in a cloud-based infrastructure, orchestration ensures that new virtual machines are provisioned, configured, and connected to the correct network resources in the correct sequence. This orchestration ensures that each service, application, and device is brought online with the proper configurations and dependencies in place, making sure that there are no errors or delays during the process.

In configuration management, the integration of automation and orchestration also supports continuous integration and continuous delivery (CI/CD) pipelines. As organizations increasingly adopt DevOps practices, automating the deployment of configurations has become a critical part of software development and infrastructure management. By automating the configuration of servers, storage, and network devices, organizations can ensure that environments are quickly set up to support the development and testing of new applications. Orchestrating this automation ensures that configurations are deployed across different environments, from development and testing to staging and production, in a consistent and reliable manner. This integration allows for faster software releases, more efficient system scaling, and improved security, as all environments are automatically configured to meet organizational standards and policies.

Automation and orchestration are particularly beneficial in dynamic environments, such as those involving cloud infrastructure and containerized applications. In traditional on-premises networks, configuration management often relied on static configurations that were manually applied and maintained. However, in cloud environments, where virtual machines, containers, and services can be rapidly created and destroyed, automation and orchestration are necessary to handle the dynamic nature of these environments. For example, container orchestration tools such as Kubernetes allow administrators to define the desired state of a containerized application, automatically deploying the required containers, ensuring that the configurations are correct, and scaling the application as demand increases. In cloud environments, configuration management tools integrated with orchestration frameworks can provision new virtual machines, apply the necessary configurations, and link them with other services in real-time, all without manual intervention.

In addition to simplifying the management of large-scale, dynamic environments, automation and orchestration tools also contribute to enhanced security. Security is a critical aspect of configuration management, as misconfigurations can open the door to vulnerabilities and attacks. Automation can help enforce security policies by ensuring that every device is consistently configured according to predefined security standards. For example, automated patch management ensures that all systems are updated with the latest security patches without requiring administrators to manually intervene. Orchestration ensures that all security services, such as firewalls, intrusion detection systems, and monitoring services, are properly configured and coordinated. By automating security tasks and ensuring the proper configuration of security tools, organizations can reduce the risk of breaches and improve their overall security posture.

Moreover, automation and orchestration allow for better monitoring and feedback during the configuration process. By automating the monitoring of systems and services, administrators can receive real-time updates on the status of devices, the success or failure of configuration changes, and the overall health of the network.

Orchestration tools provide administrators with insights into how tasks are being executed across the infrastructure, alerting them to any failures or inconsistencies. This ability to monitor and track the progress of automated processes in real-time enhances the transparency and accountability of configuration management efforts, making it easier for administrators to address issues before they affect performance or security.

One of the challenges of using automation and orchestration in configuration management is the complexity of managing large, distributed systems. The more systems and devices that are involved, the more difficult it becomes to ensure that all components are properly configured and managed. However, advanced automation and orchestration tools have been designed to handle these complexities by offering powerful features such as declarative configuration languages, version control, and rollback capabilities. By specifying the desired state of the system in code, administrators can ensure that the system is always aligned with the desired configuration, regardless of the size or complexity of the network. These tools also allow for easier troubleshooting, as configuration changes are tracked and can be rolled back if necessary.

The integration of automation and orchestration into configuration management has revolutionized how organizations manage their networks and systems. With the increasing demand for agility, scalability, and security, these tools have become indispensable for modern network and system administrators. By automating the deployment of configurations, ensuring consistency, and orchestrating the interactions between systems, organizations can improve the efficiency, security, and reliability of their IT environments. Automation and orchestration have become integral to achieving the speed and flexibility required to meet the demands of today's dynamic, fast-moving business landscape.

Scalability Considerations for Configuration Management Protocols

In the world of IT infrastructure, scalability is a critical factor for ensuring that systems can grow and adapt to increasing demands without compromising performance, security, or reliability. Configuration management protocols, which are used to maintain and apply consistent configurations across network devices, servers, and services, must be scalable to meet the needs of modern, dynamic environments. As networks grow in size and complexity, the challenges of managing configurations across a larger number of devices become more pronounced. Configuration management protocols must therefore be designed to scale efficiently, ensuring that organizations can continue to manage their infrastructure effectively as it expands.

Scalability in configuration management involves several factors, including the ability to handle an increasing number of devices, services, or systems, the capacity to manage growing amounts of configuration data, and the efficiency of applying changes to large-scale environments. As organizations scale their infrastructure, they may move from managing a handful of servers and devices to overseeing hundreds or even thousands of devices across multiple locations, cloud environments, and hybrid infrastructures. In such environments, configuration management protocols must be able to handle this growth while maintaining consistency, reducing overhead, and minimizing errors. Scalability is not only about the number of devices but also about maintaining efficient processes, ensuring that updates, configurations, and changes are applied seamlessly, regardless of the network's size.

One of the first considerations for scalability in configuration management protocols is the ability to handle a large number of devices. As networks expand, administrators may need to manage devices that are geographically dispersed, operating across different data centers, or deployed in multiple cloud environments. Managing configurations manually in such environments becomes impractical and inefficient. Protocols such as Ansible, Puppet, and Chef have been designed to scale in large environments by automating the configuration management process. These tools allow administrators to define configuration templates or playbooks that can be applied across thousands of devices at once, reducing the time and effort required to manage the growing infrastructure. The ability to push configurations simultaneously to multiple devices ensures consistency and reduces the risk of human error, which is particularly critical when managing large networks.

In highly dynamic environments, where devices are frequently added, removed, or reconfigured, scalability considerations must also take into account the ability to manage configurations dynamically. For example, cloud environments and containerized infrastructures, such as those using Kubernetes, often involve rapidly changing numbers of virtual machines or containers. Configuration management protocols must be able to dynamically provision configurations as new instances are spun up and deprovision them as old instances are shut down. Traditional configuration management methods that rely on static configurations are ill-suited for these environments. Instead, modern tools and protocols allow for the use of infrastructure as code (IaC), enabling administrators to define and manage configurations dynamically and programmatically. These tools can automatically detect new devices or services and apply the appropriate configurations in real time, ensuring that configurations are always up-to-date as the infrastructure evolves.

Another key aspect of scalability in configuration management is the ability to manage growing amounts of configuration data. As organizations scale, the complexity of their configuration files often increases as well. For example, a network of a few devices may require simple configuration files, but as the number of devices grows, the configuration files may become more complex, with a larger number of parameters, settings, and variables. The ability to efficiently manage and deploy these more complex configurations is critical for maintaining operational efficiency and consistency. Configuration management tools must therefore be designed to handle large-scale, complex configuration files without introducing significant overhead or delays. This requires the use of optimized data structures and algorithms that can efficiently process and deploy large configuration datasets.

For configuration management to be truly scalable, it is also important to consider the management of updates and changes across large infrastructures. As the size and complexity of networks grow, the process of applying configuration changes must be done in a way that minimizes downtime and avoids errors. When updating configurations across thousands of devices, administrators must ensure that changes are applied in a controlled manner, without introducing inconsistencies or conflicts. One of the most significant challenges is ensuring that changes are propagated correctly and uniformly across all devices. In a large-scale environment, even a small misconfiguration can have far-reaching consequences, such as network outages, security vulnerabilities, or performance issues. Scalable configuration management protocols must incorporate mechanisms for validating changes before they are deployed, testing them in a controlled environment, and rolling back changes if necessary.

Automation plays a vital role in ensuring the scalability of configuration management protocols. By automating repetitive tasks such as the deployment of updates, security patches, or configuration changes, administrators can ensure that these tasks are executed consistently across all devices, regardless of the network size. Automation reduces the time and effort required for manual interventions and minimizes the risk of human error. Furthermore, it allows organizations to scale their infrastructure without the need to significantly increase administrative resources. Automation also enables the continuous monitoring and auditing of configurations, ensuring that any discrepancies or deviations from the desired configuration state are detected and addressed in real time.

However, scalability is not just about managing more devices or applying configuration changes efficiently. It also involves ensuring that configuration management protocols can integrate seamlessly with other systems, services, and tools within the infrastructure. As organizations scale, they often adopt a variety of third-party tools for monitoring, security, and performance management. Configuration management protocols must be able to integrate with these tools to provide a holistic view of the network's health and performance. For example, integrating configuration management with monitoring tools allows administrators to receive real-time feedback on the status of devices and configurations, enabling them to quickly detect and address issues. Additionally, by integrating with version control systems, configuration management protocols can track changes over time, providing a history of configurations and ensuring that updates are applied in a controlled and auditable manner.

The role of cloud computing in scalability considerations is also worth noting. Cloud platforms such as AWS, Azure, and Google Cloud have become central to modern infrastructure, enabling organizations to scale their resources dynamically based on demand. Configuration management protocols must be designed to integrate with cloud platforms to manage configurations across cloud-based resources effectively. This integration ensures that configurations are applied consistently across cloud services, virtual machines, containers, and other resources. In multi-cloud or hybrid environments, scalability is even more critical, as configurations must be managed across multiple cloud providers and on-premises infrastructure. Scalable configuration management protocols ensure that these configurations are applied uniformly, regardless of the underlying platform.

Performance is another factor that cannot be overlooked when considering scalability in configuration management. As the number of devices or services increases, the time it takes to apply configurations must remain manageable. Scalable configuration management protocols must be optimized to minimize the overhead introduced during configuration deployment. This includes efficient data transfer mechanisms, parallel processing of configuration tasks, and minimizing network traffic. The ability to apply configurations quickly and without unnecessary delays is essential for maintaining operational efficiency and ensuring that services remain available during updates.

Scalability considerations for configuration management protocols are critical to ensuring that organizations can grow their networks and infrastructures without sacrificing performance, security, or reliability. The ability to manage an increasing number of devices, handle complex configurations, automate tasks, and integrate with other systems allows organizations to maintain control over their infrastructure as it expands. Whether managing devices on-premises or in the cloud, scalable configuration management protocols ensure that systems remain consistent, secure, and optimized, even as network environments become more complex. By addressing these scalability concerns, organizations can continue to adapt to changing business needs while maintaining a stable and efficient infrastructure.

Configuration Management and Network Security: Balancing Efficiency and Protection

In today's interconnected world, network security is paramount. As cyber threats evolve in complexity and sophistication, organizations must implement robust strategies to protect their networks from a variety of potential attacks. One of the most critical elements of network security is configuration management. Effective configuration management ensures that all devices and systems within a network are properly configured, up-to-date, and aligned with security best practices. However, achieving a balance between the efficiency of configuration management and the need for network security can be challenging. On one hand, administrators must ensure that configurations are applied quickly and consistently across a vast array of devices. On the other hand, they must also ensure that these configurations do not inadvertently create vulnerabilities that could be exploited by malicious actors.

Network security relies heavily on proper configuration. Misconfigurations are one of the leading causes of security breaches. A small mistake in a firewall rule, the omission of a security patch, or an improperly configured router can leave a network open to attack. Configuration management protocols play a vital role in reducing the risk of such errors. By automating the deployment of configurations and ensuring that they adhere to predefined standards, organizations can minimize the chances of misconfigurations that could compromise security. Furthermore, configuration management tools allow for the enforcement of security policies across the network, ensuring that devices are consistently configured in a secure manner. These tools also provide mechanisms for auditing and verifying configurations, helping administrators detect vulnerabilities or deviations from established security protocols.

However, the efficient management of configurations often comes at odds with the need for robust security controls. Network administrators are tasked with balancing the demands of efficiency and security, as applying configurations too quickly or broadly can lead to the introduction of vulnerabilities. For example, automated deployment tools that push configurations to a large number of devices without proper validation or testing can inadvertently deploy insecure settings across the network. Similarly, configurations that prioritize speed and convenience—such as open ports for remote management or weak password policies for easier access—can undermine the security posture of the network. While automation and efficiency are essential for managing large-scale networks, administrators must take care to ensure that these tools are used in a way that does not compromise security.

One of the main challenges in achieving this balance is the complexity of modern networks. Networks today are increasingly dynamic, with a mix of physical devices, virtual machines, cloud resources, and containerized applications. Each of these components has its own unique configuration requirements and security considerations. A configuration change that is appropriate for one device or system may not be suitable for another. For example, the configuration of a web server may require different security settings compared to a database server. Similarly, configurations for devices running in a public cloud environment must adhere to different security policies compared to those on-premises. Configuration management tools must be flexible enough to accommodate these differences, applying the right configuration to the right device while still ensuring that security standards are met.

Moreover, as networks grow, they become increasingly complex and harder to monitor. This complexity presents a significant challenge for network security. Configuration management tools must be able to scale to handle the increasing number of devices, services, and configurations, while still maintaining security. For large-scale networks, it is essential to automate the configuration of devices and services, applying updates, patches, and security settings consistently across the network. However, as automation is implemented to increase efficiency, it is crucial to ensure that proper security controls are in place to monitor these changes and detect any potential vulnerabilities. Failure to do so can lead to the rapid propagation of misconfigurations, increasing the risk of a widespread security incident.

Additionally, continuous monitoring and feedback are crucial in maintaining the balance between configuration management and network security. Configuration management tools can be integrated with monitoring systems to provide real-time visibility into the status of devices and configurations. By continuously monitoring devices for signs of misconfiguration or security vulnerabilities, administrators can identify and address issues before they result in security breaches. Monitoring systems can also provide alerts when configurations deviate from predefined security standards or when unauthorized changes are detected. This real-time feedback allows administrators to respond quickly, correcting misconfigurations and ensuring that security policies are enforced consistently across the network.

Another consideration in the balance between efficiency and security is compliance with industry regulations and security standards. Organizations in regulated industries, such as finance, healthcare, and government, must adhere to strict security policies and regulatory requirements. These regulations often dictate specific configuration settings and security measures that must be implemented to protect sensitive data. Configuration management tools can help organizations automate the enforcement of these regulations, ensuring that configurations align with compliance standards. However, the challenge lies in ensuring that the automation of configuration management does not sacrifice the thoroughness required for regulatory compliance. For example, when pushing out configuration updates across multiple devices, it is essential to verify that the changes meet all regulatory requirements before deployment.

One way to mitigate the risk of security breaches while maintaining efficiency is through the implementation of a layered security approach. This approach involves combining multiple layers of security controls to ensure that vulnerabilities are addressed from various angles. For example, in addition to configuring devices with strong security settings, administrators can use network segmentation to limit the impact of any potential breaches. By separating critical systems from less sensitive devices and enforcing strict access controls, the network can be protected even if a misconfiguration or security vulnerability exists. Similarly, implementing network monitoring tools that continuously assess the security posture of devices can add an extra layer of protection, allowing administrators to detect and respond to issues before they escalate into serious threats.

Another important strategy in balancing efficiency with security in configuration management is the use of a comprehensive change management process. Changes to network configurations should not be made haphazardly or without proper oversight. A change management process ensures that all changes are reviewed, tested, and validated before they are applied to production systems. This process helps prevent the introduction of errors or vulnerabilities while maintaining the speed and efficiency of configuration management. Automated testing tools can be used to validate configurations before they are deployed, ensuring that they meet both functional and security requirements. Additionally, change management processes provide an audit trail, allowing administrators to track the history of configuration changes and identify the source of any issues that arise.

Ultimately, finding the right balance between configuration management efficiency and network security is a continuous process. As networks grow and become more complex, the tools and strategies used to manage configurations must evolve to keep up with changing demands. Automation and orchestration are crucial to achieving efficiency in modern IT environments, but they must be implemented with caution to avoid compromising security. By integrating continuous monitoring, automated validation, and strong access controls into the configuration management process, organizations can achieve the balance needed to keep their networks secure and efficient. As cyber threats continue to evolve, the role of configuration management in maintaining a secure network environment will only become more important.

Monitoring and Auditing Configuration Changes in Network Devices

In modern network environments, the configuration of devices plays a crucial role in maintaining performance, security, and overall operational efficiency. Network devices such as routers, switches, firewalls, and load balancers are all essential components that control the flow of data and protect the network from various threats. As organizations grow and their networks become more complex, the ability to monitor and audit configuration changes in network devices becomes increasingly important. Monitoring and auditing configuration changes ensure that devices remain aligned with security policies, operational standards, and regulatory requirements. Furthermore, they provide network administrators with the tools needed to detect unauthorized changes, identify potential vulnerabilities, and maintain network stability.

Network devices are typically subject to frequent configuration changes, whether due to regular updates, new feature implementations, or troubleshooting efforts. These changes can have a significant impact on the performance and security of the network. For example, a minor misconfiguration on a firewall could inadvertently expose sensitive data to unauthorized users, or a change to a router's settings could lead to routing loops that degrade network performance. Given the critical nature of network configurations, it is essential for administrators to monitor these changes in real-time and maintain detailed records of all modifications. This ensures that any issues that arise can be traced back to their source and rectified before they escalate into more serious problems.

Monitoring configuration changes involves tracking and observing the actions taken by network administrators or automated systems when they modify device settings. Network monitoring tools, integrated with configuration management systems, can provide real-time alerts whenever a change is made. These tools continuously scan the network and track configuration alterations, reporting any deviations from predefined standards or security policies. By monitoring configuration changes in real time, administrators can quickly identify and respond to unauthorized changes or potential errors that could compromise the security or stability of the network.

Auditing, on the other hand, involves the process of reviewing and documenting all configuration changes over a given period of time. An audit trail provides a historical record of who made changes, when they were made, and what specific modifications were implemented. Auditing is particularly important in environments where regulatory compliance is required, such as healthcare, finance, or government sectors. Many regulatory frameworks, including HIPAA, PCI DSS, and GDPR, mandate that organizations maintain detailed logs of configuration changes to ensure that proper security controls are in place. Regular auditing helps verify that configuration changes are in line with compliance requirements and organizational policies. Furthermore, it allows administrators to identify trends, detect unusual activity, and ensure that the network remains secure and operational.

The auditing process typically involves logging all configuration changes made to network devices, such as firmware updates, security patches, or changes to access control lists (ACLs). Logs should capture key details, including the name of the administrator who made the change, the device affected, the specific configuration change, and the time of modification. Logs can be stored in centralized systems for easy access and long-term retention. Many configuration management tools, such as Ansible, Puppet, and Chef, provide built-in logging features that allow for automated capture of these details. These logs are invaluable for troubleshooting and forensic investigations in the event of a network incident, such as a security breach or performance degradation. By reviewing the audit logs, administrators can trace back to the source of the problem and take corrective action.

One of the key aspects of monitoring and auditing configuration changes is the ability to enforce and maintain compliance with security policies. In many cases, organizations define a set of configuration standards that must be followed across all network devices. These standards often include guidelines on encryption, access control, patch management, and firewall configurations. Monitoring tools can be configured to continuously check device configurations against these standards, flagging any deviations from the expected configuration.

For example, if a firewall rule is modified to allow access to a previously restricted network segment, the monitoring system can flag this change as a potential security risk. Auditing these changes then allows administrators to review whether the modification was authorized and, if necessary, revert the configuration to its secure state.

Effective auditing also plays a critical role in detecting malicious activity within the network. Cyber attackers often exploit misconfigurations or make unauthorized changes to network devices in an attempt to gain access to sensitive information or disrupt services. Regular auditing of configuration changes provides a means of detecting such attempts early. By monitoring the frequency and nature of configuration changes, network administrators can identify suspicious patterns or activities, such as unauthorized access to a device or changes to critical security settings. For example, if an employee with limited access rights attempts to modify configurations on a sensitive network device, the auditing system can alert the administrator to the unauthorized change. This early detection can help prevent further security incidents and mitigate potential damage.

In large-scale networks, the complexity of tracking and auditing configuration changes increases significantly. Networks often consist of numerous devices spread across different locations, and configurations may be modified by multiple administrators or automated systems. To ensure that configuration changes are properly managed, organizations often implement centralized configuration management and monitoring systems. These systems aggregate logs from all network devices, providing a single point of visibility for administrators. Centralized systems also allow for the automation of configuration checks, alerts, and audits, ensuring that devices are continuously monitored and any deviations from established configurations are flagged in real time.

Moreover, integration with other network management systems enhances the effectiveness of configuration change monitoring and auditing. By combining configuration management tools with network performance monitoring, vulnerability scanning, and security information and event management (SIEM) systems, administrators can gain a more comprehensive view of network health and security. For example, network monitoring systems can track device performance and alert administrators to performance issues or network congestion, while configuration management tools ensure that devices are configured correctly and in compliance with security policies. Integration with SIEM systems further strengthens security by correlating configuration changes with other security events, allowing administrators to detect patterns of suspicious behavior and respond proactively.

The automation of configuration management and auditing processes is a critical step in improving efficiency and accuracy. Manual tracking of configuration changes across a large network is labor-intensive and prone to human error. Automation tools help streamline the process, reducing the burden on administrators and ensuring consistency across all devices. Automated systems can monitor configurations in real time, automatically log changes, and trigger alerts when changes deviate from predefined policies. Additionally, automated auditing can generate regular reports that provide insights into compliance status, making it easier for organizations to meet regulatory requirements and maintain a secure network environment.

In conclusion, monitoring and auditing configuration changes in network devices are essential practices for maintaining network security, operational stability, and compliance with regulatory standards. By tracking and documenting configuration changes, administrators can ensure that devices are configured securely and consistently, while also detecting potential vulnerabilities or unauthorized actions. The use of centralized tools, automated systems, and integration with other network management platforms further enhances the efficiency and effectiveness of these processes. As networks continue to grow in complexity, the ability to monitor and audit configuration changes in real time will remain a critical component of a robust network management strategy.

Configuration Management Protocols in Large-Scale Enterprise Networks

In large-scale enterprise networks, configuration management protocols play a vital role in ensuring that network devices, systems, and services are set up, maintained, and updated efficiently. As enterprise networks grow in size and complexity, managing configurations manually becomes increasingly impractical and error-prone. In such environments, configuration management protocols provide the automation, consistency, and scalability needed to manage devices across multiple locations, data centers, and cloud environments. These protocols not only streamline network operations but also enhance security, performance, and compliance, all while reducing the risk of downtime or service disruptions.

Large-scale enterprise networks typically consist of thousands of network devices, ranging from routers and switches to firewalls, load balancers, and security appliances. As these devices are deployed across a wide array of physical and virtual environments, each with its own set of requirements, configuration management becomes a critical task. The configuration of each device must be carefully controlled to ensure it aligns with organizational policies, security standards, and operational goals. Configuration management protocols help automate the process of configuring these devices, making it possible to deploy consistent configurations across a vast network without the need for manual intervention.

One of the primary advantages of using configuration management protocols in large-scale networks is automation. Automation significantly reduces the time and effort required to configure network devices, ensuring that devices are provisioned and updated in accordance with predefined standards. Tools such as Ansible, Puppet, Chef, and SaltStack have been designed to automate the deployment of configuration files and system updates across thousands of devices, reducing the risk of misconfigurations and human error. With these tools, network administrators can define configurations in code, which can then be automatically applied to all devices in the network. This eliminates the need for manual intervention, ensuring that configuration changes are applied consistently and without delay, even across large and distributed environments.

In addition to improving efficiency, automation through configuration management protocols also enhances consistency. In large enterprise networks, it is common for multiple administrators to be involved in configuring different devices. Without automated tools, there is a high risk of inconsistency, where devices in different locations or departments may have different configurations, even though they are meant to serve the same purpose. Such inconsistencies can lead to network performance issues, security vulnerabilities, or compliance violations. By using configuration management protocols, administrators can ensure that all devices receive the same configuration settings, making the network more predictable and stable. This is particularly important when applying security patches or updates, as it ensures that every device in the network is configured in the same secure manner.

Security is another key aspect of configuration management in large-scale networks. Misconfigurations are one of the leading causes of security vulnerabilities, and large networks are especially susceptible to this risk. A small error in the configuration of a single device, such as a misconfigured firewall rule or an exposed port, can provide attackers with a way to exploit the network. Configuration management protocols help mitigate this risk by ensuring that security settings are consistently applied across the network. For instance, network administrators can define security policies, such as encryption standards, access controls, and firewall configurations, and ensure that these policies are applied uniformly across all devices. Automated tools can also verify that configurations adhere to these security policies, reducing the likelihood of vulnerabilities caused by human error or outdated configurations.

Scalability is a major consideration when managing configurations in large-scale enterprise networks. As networks expand, the number of devices that need to be configured, monitored, and maintained grows exponentially. Without scalable configuration management protocols, managing this growth becomes increasingly difficult. Configuration management tools must be capable of handling large volumes of configuration data, applying changes to thousands of devices, and managing configurations in dynamic environments. Cloud-based environments, containerized systems, and virtual machines further complicate this challenge, as configurations must be applied across diverse platforms and technologies. Cloud integration within configuration management protocols ensures that the network remains scalable, as it allows administrators to define and deploy configurations across hybrid environments that include both on-premises and cloud-based resources.

Moreover, large-scale enterprise networks often span multiple geographical locations, which presents additional challenges for configuration management. Network devices are often deployed across different regions, countries, or even continents, requiring configuration management protocols to be able to handle devices in various time zones, regions, and regulatory environments. In such cases, configuration management tools can centralize control over all network devices, allowing administrators to deploy changes and updates remotely and consistently. This centralization not only streamlines the management process but also ensures that administrators can maintain full visibility and control over the entire network, regardless of the geographical distribution of the devices.

The integration of configuration management protocols with other network management tools is another critical factor for large-scale networks. In complex network environments, configuration management is just one part of the overall network management process. To optimize network performance and security, configuration management tools must be integrated with monitoring systems, incident response tools, and vulnerability scanning software. By doing so, administrators can receive real-time feedback on the status of network devices and configurations, enabling them to identify issues and apply fixes more quickly. For example, if a vulnerability is detected on a device, the configuration management protocol can be used to automatically apply the necessary security patches or updates, ensuring that the network remains secure and compliant.

Another important consideration is compliance with industry regulations and internal policies. In regulated industries, such as healthcare, finance, and telecommunications, organizations must ensure that their network configurations comply with specific security and privacy standards. Configuration management protocols help automate the enforcement of these regulations by applying predefined security settings and configuration standards across the network. Compliance auditing tools integrated with configuration management systems can track and log all configuration changes, providing an audit trail that demonstrates adherence to regulatory requirements. This is particularly useful during audits, as administrators can quickly generate reports showing that devices have been configured in accordance with applicable standards and regulations.

Furthermore, the ability to perform rollback operations is essential in large-scale networks. When applying configuration changes, there is always a risk that the changes will cause unforeseen issues or disrupt network operations. In such cases, being able to quickly revert to a previous configuration is critical for minimizing downtime and restoring network functionality. Many configuration management protocols include version control and rollback features that allow administrators to restore previous configurations with minimal effort. This ability to quickly recover from configuration errors ensures that the network remains resilient and reduces the risk of service interruptions caused by incorrect configuration changes.

As networks continue to evolve, the role of configuration management protocols in large-scale enterprise networks will only become more important. These protocols provide the automation, scalability, security, and consistency needed to manage complex, dynamic environments. By ensuring that devices are properly configured and maintained, network administrators can ensure that their infrastructure remains stable, secure, and compliant with organizational and regulatory requirements. Through the use of advanced configuration management tools, enterprises can efficiently manage the ever-growing complexity of their networks, enabling them to adapt to new technologies, scale their operations, and maintain optimal network performance.

Redundancy and Failover Strategies for Configuration Management Protocols

In the modern era of networking and IT infrastructure, ensuring the continuity and availability of services is crucial for maintaining a reliable and secure environment. One of the primary challenges faced by network administrators is ensuring that configuration management systems remain operational even in the event of hardware failures, network disruptions, or system outages. This is where redundancy and failover strategies come into play. Redundancy refers to the practice of duplicating critical systems or components to ensure that there is no single point of failure, while failover strategies define the automatic switching to backup systems when a failure is detected. Together, these strategies play an essential role in maintaining the stability and reliability of configuration management protocols, particularly in large and complex networks where downtime can have a significant impact on operations.

Configuration management protocols are responsible for ensuring that all devices in a network are configured correctly and remain consistent with security policies, operational standards, and performance requirements. However, if the system that manages these configurations becomes unavailable due to a failure, the entire network could be compromised. This can lead to delays in deploying updates, inconsistent configurations, and even security vulnerabilities. By implementing redundancy and failover strategies, organizations can ensure that their configuration management systems remain operational at all times, even in the face of hardware or software failures.

One of the primary methods for achieving redundancy in configuration management systems is through the use of backup servers and high-availability (HA) setups. By deploying redundant servers that replicate the primary configuration management server, organizations can ensure that if one server fails, the backup server can take over and continue to manage the configurations without interruption. This setup is especially important for large-scale environments where configuration changes need to be applied rapidly across many devices. If the primary server becomes unavailable, the backup server can immediately step in, ensuring that there is no disruption in the configuration process. These redundant servers can be placed in geographically distributed locations to avoid risks associated with local outages, such as power failures or natural disasters.

In addition to having backup servers, ensuring that data is replicated and synchronized across multiple locations is another important aspect of redundancy in configuration management systems. This involves creating real-time copies of configuration files, scripts, and deployment templates so that they are always available, regardless of where the failure occurs. With synchronized data, administrators can easily recover lost information, minimize the chances of configuration data corruption, and ensure that configuration management tasks can continue without data loss. Replicating configuration data to multiple locations also ensures that administrators can access the system from various points in the network, which can be particularly useful for geographically dispersed teams or in cloud-based environments.

Failover strategies are an essential component of redundancy, ensuring that the configuration management system can quickly switch to backup systems in the event of a failure. These strategies can be implemented using a variety of methods, from automated software-based solutions to hardware-based load balancers. Automated failover systems continuously monitor the health of configuration management servers, checking for any signs of failure such as server crashes, network disruptions, or application errors. If a failure is detected, the system automatically reroutes traffic to the backup server or resource without requiring human intervention. This automation ensures that the failover process is seamless, reducing downtime and minimizing the impact of the failure on network operations.

Another important failover strategy is load balancing, which can be used in combination with redundancy to improve the performance and availability of configuration management systems. Load balancers distribute network traffic across multiple servers, preventing any single server from becoming overwhelmed with requests. In the context of configuration management, load balancing ensures that configuration requests are distributed evenly across the system, improving performance and reducing the likelihood of service disruptions. If one server fails, the load balancer can redirect traffic to the remaining operational servers, ensuring that configuration management tasks can continue uninterrupted. Load balancing also allows organizations to scale their configuration management infrastructure as needed, adding additional servers to handle increased traffic or workload demands.

For cloud-based environments, redundancy and failover strategies are particularly important due to the dynamic nature of cloud computing. Cloud providers, such as AWS, Azure, and Google Cloud, offer a variety of tools and services to support high availability and disaster recovery, making it easier to implement redundancy and failover strategies for configuration management systems. Cloud-based configuration management solutions, such as those integrated with platform-as-a-service (PaaS) or container orchestration platforms like Kubernetes, allow for automated failover and scaling. These solutions can detect when a node or service fails and automatically deploy resources to maintain configuration management capabilities. Cloud environments provide the added benefit of being able to quickly provision new resources to handle increased demand or recovery after a failure, without the need for significant manual intervention.

In addition to automated failover systems, organizations must ensure that their backup systems are properly tested and validated. Redundant systems and failover mechanisms are only effective if they are regularly tested to ensure that they will function properly when needed. Organizations should perform regular failover tests to verify that the backup systems are operational and capable of handling the load in the event of a failure. These tests should simulate various types of failures, such as server crashes, network outages, or service interruptions, to ensure that the failover process works smoothly and that all configuration management tasks can continue without disruption. By conducting these tests periodically, organizations can identify and address potential weaknesses in their failover strategies before they become critical issues.

Another important aspect of redundancy and failover strategies is the monitoring of configuration management systems. Continuous monitoring ensures that any issues or potential failures are detected before they can impact the network. Monitoring tools track the health and performance of configuration management servers, alerting administrators to any problems that might lead to a failure. By integrating monitoring with redundancy and failover systems, administrators can ensure that they are notified in real-time when a failure occurs, allowing them to take corrective action immediately. Monitoring also provides valuable insights into the performance and reliability of the configuration management system, helping administrators identify potential bottlenecks or areas for improvement.

Redundancy and failover strategies are not only critical for maintaining the availability of configuration management systems but also for improving network security. A configuration management system that is down or compromised can lead to serious security vulnerabilities, as devices may not be updated with the latest patches or configuration changes. By ensuring that these systems are always available, organizations can ensure that security configurations are applied consistently across all devices and that any new security patches are deployed without delay. Moreover, a well-implemented failover system ensures that in the event of a security breach or attack, the configuration management system can continue to operate securely, allowing administrators to take action to contain the breach and recover quickly.

As organizations continue to expand their networks and adopt more complex infrastructures, redundancy and failover strategies will only become more important for maintaining the availability, performance, and security of configuration management systems. These strategies ensure that organizations can continue to manage and deploy configurations efficiently, even in the face of unexpected failures or disruptions. By combining redundancy, automated failover, load balancing, and continuous monitoring, organizations can create a robust and resilient configuration management system that ensures uninterrupted service and optimal network performance.

Overcoming Network Challenges in Configuration Management Protocols

In the realm of network management, configuration management protocols are fundamental to ensuring that devices, services, and systems are correctly set up and maintained. However, as networks become more complex, with diverse devices, software, and technologies, network administrators face several challenges in applying and managing these configurations. From dealing with inconsistent network topologies to managing configurations across distributed systems, the road to effective configuration management is fraught with difficulties. Overcoming these challenges requires a deep understanding of the infrastructure, careful planning, and the right set of tools to ensure configurations are applied consistently and efficiently across a growing and increasingly dynamic network environment.

One of the most significant challenges in network configuration management is the sheer complexity of modern networks. Networks today span multiple physical and virtual environments, with devices ranging from routers and switches to cloud-based services, containers, and Internet of Things (IoT) devices. Each of these devices may require unique configurations, which must be applied while maintaining consistency across the entire network. Managing configurations for such diverse systems can be particularly challenging, as it requires network administrators to ensure that all devices adhere to common security policies, operational standards, and performance requirements. Without the proper tools, it is easy for configurations to become inconsistent across different devices, which can lead to network disruptions, security vulnerabilities, or compliance issues.

To overcome the complexity of managing configurations across diverse environments, administrators must employ configuration management protocols that offer automation and flexibility. Automation is crucial in reducing the administrative burden and eliminating the potential for human error. Tools like Ansible, Puppet, Chef, and SaltStack enable administrators to automate the deployment of configurations across thousands of devices, whether they are physical devices or virtual machines in the cloud. By defining configuration templates, these tools ensure that all devices in the network are consistently configured according to predefined standards, regardless of their type or location. Automated configuration management also allows administrators to apply updates, patches, and changes across the network quickly and reliably, reducing the risk of downtime or misconfiguration.

Another challenge faced by network administrators in large-scale environments is the management of network changes in real-time. Networks are constantly evolving, with new devices and services being added, existing devices being reconfigured, and software updates being deployed. In dynamic environments such as cloud infrastructures or containerized applications, it can be difficult to ensure that configurations are always aligned with the desired state of the network. Network administrators must be able to manage configurations in real-time, applying changes quickly and accurately to keep up with the ever-changing network landscape.

Real-time configuration management protocols address this challenge by allowing administrators to automate configuration updates as soon as a change is needed. In cloud-based networks, where instances are provisioned and decommissioned at a rapid pace, real-time management ensures that newly provisioned devices receive the correct configurations immediately. Configuration management tools integrated with cloud services, such as AWS CloudFormation or Azure Resource Manager, allow administrators to define infrastructure as code (IaC), making it possible to automatically configure and deploy resources as they are created. This approach ensures that the network remains consistent and secure, even as it scales and evolves.

Security is another critical concern in configuration management, especially in large-scale networks. Misconfigurations are one of the leading causes of security breaches, and ensuring that devices are configured securely is a continuous challenge for administrators. For example, improperly configured firewalls, weak passwords, or outdated security protocols can provide attackers with an opportunity to exploit vulnerabilities in the network. In large networks, manually checking each device for proper security settings is not feasible, and administrators must rely on configuration management protocols to enforce security policies across the entire infrastructure.

To overcome this challenge, administrators can use configuration management tools that integrate security best practices into the configuration process. These tools can enforce encryption standards, access control lists (ACLs), and other security measures across all network devices automatically. For example, configuration management systems can be set up to apply security patches across all devices at once, ensuring that devices remain protected from known vulnerabilities. Additionally, these tools can monitor devices for unauthorized configuration changes and alert administrators when deviations from security policies are detected. By integrating security into the configuration management process, administrators can reduce the risk of vulnerabilities and ensure that the network remains secure, even as it grows and evolves.

Network performance is also a crucial consideration when managing configurations in large-scale environments. Configuration changes can have a significant impact on network performance, particularly when dealing with large numbers of devices. A minor misconfiguration, such as an incorrectly set routing protocol or a malfunctioning load balancer, can lead to performance degradation or even network outages. In such environments, administrators need to ensure that configuration changes do not disrupt the network's performance, especially in critical applications or services.

To address this challenge, administrators must employ configuration management protocols that not only automate the deployment of configurations but also validate the performance impact of these changes. Some tools allow administrators to test configuration changes in staging environments before they are deployed in production, reducing the risk of performance issues. Additionally, configuration management protocols can be integrated with performance monitoring tools to provide real-time feedback on the impact of configuration changes. By monitoring the performance of the network and detecting issues early, administrators can ensure that configuration changes do not disrupt network operations.

One of the most challenging aspects of configuration management in large-scale networks is dealing with network devices that are geographically dispersed. In such environments, configuration management protocols must be capable of handling devices across multiple data centers, branch offices, or remote locations. Managing devices in different regions or countries requires careful coordination to ensure that configuration changes are applied consistently and securely, regardless of the device's physical location. Furthermore, these devices may operate in different time zones or be subject to local regulatory requirements, which can complicate configuration management even further.

To overcome this challenge, configuration management tools can be configured to manage devices in different locations by centralizing control and providing visibility into all devices in the network. By using centralized configuration management systems, administrators can apply configurations to devices across multiple regions from a single interface. Additionally, these systems can be integrated with cloud-based solutions that offer scalable, flexible management of distributed networks. In multi-cloud or hybrid environments, configuration management protocols that support diverse platforms and technologies can ensure that configurations are applied uniformly across all environments.

Finally, as networks become more complex, the challenge of managing configuration drift becomes more pronounced. Configuration drift occurs when a device's configuration diverges from the desired state due to manual changes, updates, or errors. This can lead to inconsistencies, security vulnerabilities, or performance issues. In large networks, tracking and correcting configuration drift manually is virtually impossible, making automated configuration management essential.

To address configuration drift, network administrators can use configuration management tools that continuously monitor devices for deviations from the desired configuration state. These tools can automatically correct any discrepancies, ensuring that devices remain aligned with organizational policies and standards. By providing real-time visibility into configuration states, administrators can quickly detect and fix configuration drift, maintaining consistency and reducing the risk of security or performance issues.

The challenges of managing configurations in large-scale networks are complex, but with the right tools and strategies, they can be effectively overcome. Configuration management protocols that offer automation, security, scalability, and real-time management are essential for maintaining a stable and secure network infrastructure. By automating configuration deployment, ensuring consistency across devices, and integrating security and performance monitoring, network administrators can ensure that their networks remain reliable, secure, and efficient as they scale and evolve.

Data Integrity and Verification in TFTP and SCP Transfers

In network administration, data integrity and the ability to verify the accuracy and completeness of file transfers are essential to maintaining a secure and stable network environment. Configuration files, system images, and other important data are often transferred between network devices, servers, and clients. Ensuring that these files arrive at their destination without being altered, corrupted, or compromised is a fundamental part of network security. Two common protocols used for transferring files across networks are Trivial File Transfer Protocol (TFTP) and Secure Copy Protocol (SCP). While both serve the purpose of transferring files, they differ significantly in terms of security features, data integrity checks, and verification mechanisms. Understanding how data integrity is maintained and verified in TFTP and SCP transfers is critical for network administrators who need to ensure that their transfers are reliable and secure.

TFTP, despite its simplicity and widespread use, does not include any built-in mechanisms for ensuring data integrity during file transfers. TFTP is a lightweight protocol designed for speed and simplicity, making it ideal for transferring small files, such as configuration files or boot images, within trusted local area networks (LANs). However, TFTP lacks features such as encryption, authentication, and error correction, which leaves it vulnerable to data corruption and malicious tampering during transfers. This limitation means that data integrity checks are not inherently part of the protocol itself.

To mitigate this risk, administrators must rely on external mechanisms for ensuring the integrity of the data being transferred via TFTP. One common approach is to use checksums or hash functions to validate the integrity of the transferred files. Before a file is transferred using TFTP, a checksum or hash value is generated for the original file. This value is then sent alongside the file to the receiving system. Once the transfer is complete, the receiving system generates a checksum or hash for the received file and compares it to the original value. If the two values match, the file has been transferred without corruption or alteration. If there is a mismatch, the file transfer can be deemed unreliable, and the transfer process can be retried. This simple yet effective approach helps ensure that the file being transferred is the same as the one initially sent.

For even greater confidence in data integrity, administrators can combine TFTP with more advanced network monitoring and error detection tools. These tools can detect anomalies in the file transfer process, such as network congestion or packet loss, that could lead to corrupted files. While TFTP does not natively support these advanced features, combining it with other network management tools can help mitigate the risks associated with data integrity. However, these added layers of complexity do not fully address the security shortcomings of TFTP, as the protocol itself remains unencrypted and unauthenticated.

In contrast, SCP offers more robust features for ensuring data integrity and security during file transfers. SCP, which is based on the Secure Shell (SSH) protocol, provides both encryption and authentication, which are critical for secure file transfers. Unlike TFTP, which transmits data in plaintext, SCP encrypts the data being transferred, preventing unauthorized parties from intercepting or tampering with the files during the transfer process. This encryption helps to maintain both the confidentiality and integrity of the data, ensuring that the file being transferred cannot be read or altered by third parties.

SCP also includes built-in data integrity checks as part of its design. When a file is transferred via SCP, the protocol automatically verifies the integrity of the file by using a cryptographic hash function. This process ensures that the file is not corrupted during transit and that the data received by the destination system matches the original file. SCP performs this verification by comparing the hash value of the file at the source with the hash value of the file at the destination. If the hash values match, the integrity of the file is confirmed, and the transfer is considered successful. If the values do not match, SCP will either prompt for a retry or signal an error, ensuring that corrupted or incomplete files are not accepted.

Another feature of SCP that enhances data integrity is its ability to resume interrupted transfers. If a file transfer is interrupted due to network issues or a session timeout, SCP can resume the transfer from where it left off, instead of starting the entire transfer over again. This feature helps prevent data corruption and ensures that large files are transferred reliably, even in the face of network instability. It also minimizes the chances of partial transfers, which can lead to incomplete or corrupted files being delivered.

While SCP offers more advanced security and integrity features compared to TFTP, it is not without its own limitations. SCP is typically used for transferring files between trusted systems, as it requires SSH access and authentication. This means that both the sending and receiving systems must be configured to support SSH, and users must have the necessary credentials to authenticate the connection. Additionally, SCP can be slower than TFTP due to the overhead introduced by encryption and authentication, which can be a disadvantage in environments where speed is a critical factor.

Despite these challenges, SCP is widely preferred for transferring sensitive or critical data across networks, as its robust security and data integrity features make it a safer choice than TFTP in most scenarios. SCP's ability to provide encryption, authentication, and built-in integrity checks makes it particularly useful for configurations, backups, and system updates that require both speed and security. Its ability to automatically verify the integrity of files during the transfer process gives administrators greater confidence that the data being transferred has not been compromised.

For both TFTP and SCP, it is important for administrators to monitor the transfer process and perform routine checks on the integrity of the transferred files. While TFTP can be augmented with external tools for verification, SCP's built-in features make it a more reliable choice for environments where data integrity and security are top priorities. In large-scale or distributed networks, where the volume of file transfers is high, using SCP can help prevent data loss, corruption, and unauthorized access, ensuring that configuration files, system images, and other critical data are transferred safely and accurately.

In summary, data integrity and verification are essential components of any file transfer process in network management. While TFTP offers a simple, fast solution for file transfers within trusted networks, it requires additional steps, such as checksums or external monitoring tools, to ensure data integrity. SCP, on the other hand, provides built-in encryption, authentication, and data integrity checks, making it a more secure and reliable option for transferring critical files across potentially insecure networks. By understanding the strengths and limitations of both protocols, administrators can make informed decisions about which method to use based on the specific requirements of their network and data security policies.

Configuration Management Protocols in Edge and IoT Networks

The rapid expansion of the Internet of Things (IoT) and edge computing has introduced new complexities in the world of network management. These technologies rely on a vast network of interconnected devices that collect and process data at or near the source, rather than relying on centralized cloud-based systems. While edge computing enables faster data processing and reduced latency, it also presents unique challenges for configuration management. As the number of devices grows exponentially, it becomes increasingly difficult to maintain consistent, secure, and efficient configurations across the network. Configuration management protocols play a crucial role in addressing these challenges, ensuring that devices within edge and IoT networks are properly configured, secure, and functioning optimally.

At its core, configuration management refers to the processes and tools used to manage and maintain the configuration settings of devices and systems within a network. In traditional enterprise networks, configuration management is typically applied to a relatively small number of centralized devices, such as routers, switches, and servers. However, in edge and IoT networks, the sheer scale of devices—often numbering in the thousands or even millions—requires a much more sophisticated and automated approach. Devices in these networks range from simple sensors and actuators to complex gateways and edge servers, each with its own unique configuration needs and security requirements.

One of the primary challenges in managing configurations in IoT and edge networks is the diversity of devices and operating environments. IoT devices can be highly varied, with different hardware architectures, communication protocols, and software platforms. Some devices may run on minimal hardware with limited processing power, while others may be more complex and run sophisticated applications. The diversity of devices makes it difficult to apply a one-size-fits-all configuration management approach. Configuration management protocols in edge and IoT networks must be flexible enough to accommodate this wide range of devices and environments while still ensuring that configurations are consistent, secure, and compliant with organizational policies.

To address this challenge, configuration management protocols must be able to handle heterogeneous environments and support a variety of device types, operating systems, and network architectures. Protocols such as YANG (Yet Another Next Generation) and NETCONF (Network Configuration Protocol) are increasingly being used in IoT and edge networks to manage device configurations in a standardized way. These protocols provide a way to model and manage device configurations, ensuring that devices are configured according to predefined standards. YANG, for example, allows administrators to define configuration templates for different types of devices, which can then be applied automatically using NETCONF or other management protocols. This approach ensures consistency across the network while still allowing for the customization of configurations to suit the unique needs of different devices.

In addition to flexibility, configuration management protocols in IoT and edge networks must also support automation. With the large number of devices involved, manual configuration management is no longer feasible. Automation allows network administrators to deploy and update configurations across the entire network with minimal human intervention. Automated configuration management tools can push updates and changes to devices on a scheduled basis, ensuring that all devices are kept up to date with the latest configuration settings, security patches, and software updates. Automation also helps ensure that configurations are applied consistently across the network, reducing the risk of errors or inconsistencies that could lead to security vulnerabilities or performance issues.

Security is another critical aspect of configuration management in edge and IoT networks. Given the distributed nature of these networks and the potential for devices to be deployed in remote or unsecured locations, ensuring the security of configuration data is paramount. Many IoT devices are designed with minimal security features, which can leave them vulnerable to attacks if their configurations are not properly managed. Configuration management protocols must include mechanisms to secure configuration data during transmission and storage. This can be achieved through encryption and authentication protocols, such as Transport Layer Security (TLS), which protect configuration data from being intercepted or tampered with during transfers. Additionally, ensuring that devices are regularly updated with security patches and configuration changes is essential to protect against emerging threats.

Another important security consideration is ensuring that access to device configurations is tightly controlled. In large IoT and edge networks, multiple administrators or automated systems may need to modify device configurations. To prevent unauthorized access and ensure accountability, configuration management protocols must include access control mechanisms. Role-based access control (RBAC) allows administrators to define different levels of access to configuration data, ensuring that only authorized users can modify certain settings. Additionally, audit trails can be maintained to log all changes to device configurations, providing transparency and accountability in case of security breaches or other issues.

As IoT and edge networks continue to grow, scalability becomes an increasingly important factor in configuration management. The number of devices in these networks is projected to increase exponentially, making it critical for configuration management protocols to scale efficiently. Many traditional configuration management tools are not designed to handle the scale of IoT and edge networks, which can consist of millions of devices spread across multiple geographic locations. Configuration management protocols in these networks must be able to handle this scale by supporting distributed architectures and decentralized management. By using cloud-based or hybrid management systems, network administrators can distribute the load of managing configurations across multiple servers, ensuring that the system remains responsive and efficient even as the network grows.

In addition to scalability, configuration management protocols must also be able to handle dynamic and changing network environments. In edge and IoT networks, devices are often added, removed, or reconfigured on the fly, creating a constantly evolving network landscape. Configuration management protocols must be able to accommodate these changes and ensure that devices are properly configured as they join the network or undergo updates. This requires protocols that can automatically detect new devices and apply the appropriate configurations without requiring manual intervention. Additionally, configuration management tools must be able to handle devices that may not be consistently online or accessible, such as battery-powered IoT devices in remote locations. This dynamic nature of edge and IoT networks requires flexible and responsive configuration management systems.

Moreover, ensuring that devices are continuously monitored for performance and security is a key part of configuration management in these networks. Monitoring tools integrated with configuration management systems can provide real-time feedback on the status of devices and alert administrators to any issues with configurations, such as deviations from expected settings or signs of security vulnerabilities. By continuously monitoring the performance and health of devices, administrators can quickly detect problems and take corrective action, minimizing downtime and maintaining the reliability of the network.

The complexity and scale of edge and IoT networks make configuration management a critical component of network operations. By using advanced configuration management protocols that support automation, security, flexibility, and scalability, organizations can ensure that their devices are properly configured, secure, and optimized for performance. These protocols provide the tools necessary to manage devices in highly dynamic and distributed environments, ensuring that configurations are applied consistently across the network while also accommodating the unique needs of different devices. With the growing reliance on IoT and edge computing, effective configuration management is more important than ever for maintaining the security, efficiency, and stability of modern networks.

Integrating Configuration Management with SDN (Software-Defined Networking)

The rise of Software-Defined Networking (SDN) has fundamentally transformed the way networks are designed, managed, and operated. Traditional networking models, which rely on static, hardware-based configurations, are being replaced by more flexible, programmable networks that allow for dynamic adjustments and centralized control. SDN decouples the control plane from the data plane, providing network administrators with the ability to manage network resources and policies through software rather than hardware-based configurations. As networks grow in scale and complexity, configuration management becomes increasingly critical to ensure consistency, security, and performance across SDN-enabled environments. Integrating configuration management with SDN offers the potential to streamline network operations, automate network provisioning, and simplify the management of network devices.

At its core, SDN provides a centralized controller that manages network traffic, policies, and configurations across the entire network. By using a software-driven approach, SDN enables administrators to adjust network configurations in real-time, responding to changing traffic patterns or shifting business needs. This centralized control, however, also introduces the challenge of ensuring that configurations remain consistent across a wide range of devices and systems within the network. Configuration management plays a crucial role in addressing this challenge by automating the process of applying and maintaining configurations across the network. When integrated with SDN, configuration management systems ensure that all network devices are consistently configured according to organizational policies and standards, which helps prevent misconfigurations, reduces manual intervention, and enhances network security.

One of the key benefits of integrating configuration management with SDN is the ability to automate the deployment and management of network configurations. In traditional networks, configurations must be manually applied to each device, which is time-consuming and prone to human error. This process can be especially difficult to manage in large, dynamic environments where devices are constantly being added, removed, or reconfigured. In contrast, SDN-enabled networks provide a centralized control plane that can be used to automate configuration changes across all devices simultaneously. By integrating configuration management tools such as Ansible, Puppet, or Chef with SDN controllers, administrators can automate the process of configuring network devices, applying security policies, and provisioning network services in a consistent and efficient manner.

The integration of configuration management with SDN also enables real-time adjustments to network configurations. In traditional networking models, changes to network configurations often require significant manual intervention and can take a long time to propagate across the network. With SDN, network administrators can make configuration changes in real-time, instantly applying updates to the network's behavior. This is especially useful in environments where network demands change rapidly, such as in cloud computing or data center networks. By integrating configuration management tools with SDN controllers, administrators can ensure that configuration changes are applied automatically and consistently across all devices, reducing the risk of misconfigurations and minimizing downtime. For example, when a new service needs to be deployed or network bandwidth needs to be adjusted, SDN and configuration management tools can work together to automatically adjust the configuration of network devices, ensuring that the network is always aligned with the organization's goals.

In addition to automation and real-time adjustments, configuration management integration with SDN can improve network security. As networks become more complex and dynamic, ensuring that security policies are consistently applied across all devices becomes increasingly difficult. In SDN-enabled networks, the centralized control plane provides a powerful mechanism for enforcing security policies across the network. Configuration management tools can be integrated with SDN controllers to ensure that security configurations, such as access control lists (ACLs), firewall settings, and intrusion detection systems, are applied consistently across all devices. This integration ensures that all devices in the network are configured to meet organizational security standards and compliance requirements. Moreover, by automating the application of security configurations, configuration management tools reduce the risk of human error, which can lead to vulnerabilities in the network.

The integration of configuration management with SDN also enhances network visibility and monitoring. In traditional networks, tracking configuration changes and monitoring the health of devices can be challenging, especially in large environments. By integrating configuration management systems with SDN controllers, administrators gain real-time visibility into the status of the network and the configurations of individual devices. Monitoring tools can be used to detect configuration drift, which occurs when devices fall out of alignment with the desired configuration. When configuration drift is detected, administrators can be alerted and take corrective action, ensuring that the network remains consistent and secure. Additionally, centralized monitoring and logging tools can be used to track changes to network configurations, providing an audit trail that can be used for troubleshooting, compliance reporting, or security investigations.

As SDN-enabled networks grow in scale, managing configurations across a large number of devices becomes more complex. The ability to manage configurations centrally and automate deployment is especially important in these environments. Integration with configuration management tools ensures that administrators can manage large-scale SDN environments efficiently, ensuring that configurations are consistently applied across all devices, regardless of their location. By using a combination of configuration management tools and SDN controllers, administrators can create automated workflows that allow for the rapid deployment of configurations and the scaling of network resources. This capability is particularly important in cloud data centers, where the network infrastructure is highly dynamic, and resources need to be provisioned quickly and automatically.

Another advantage of integrating configuration management with SDN is the ability to handle multi-vendor environments. In many networks, devices from multiple vendors are deployed, which can complicate configuration management. Each vendor may have its own approach to configuration and may not provide a unified management interface. By using SDN as the centralized control plane, administrators can abstract away the differences between vendor-specific devices and manage configurations in a consistent way. Configuration management tools can be integrated with SDN controllers to apply uniform configurations across devices, regardless of the vendor, ensuring that the network remains interoperable and consistent.

However, despite the numerous benefits, there are challenges associated with integrating configuration management with SDN. One of the primary challenges is the complexity of managing network policies and configurations in a dynamic environment. SDN enables real-time changes to the network, but this dynamic nature can introduce complexity when it comes to ensuring that configurations remain consistent and aligned with organizational policies. Additionally, as SDN relies on a centralized control plane, there is a risk of a single point of failure. To mitigate this risk, organizations must implement redundancy and failover strategies to ensure that the SDN controller remains operational in the event of hardware or software failures. Furthermore, ensuring that configuration management tools are properly integrated with SDN controllers and are capable of managing the full range of network devices and services is crucial for success.

The integration of configuration management protocols with SDN offers significant benefits for network administrators. By automating configuration deployment, ensuring security policy enforcement, improving network visibility, and enabling real-time adjustments, SDN and configuration management tools work together to streamline the management of modern networks. However, as networks grow in complexity, organizations must ensure that their configuration management strategies are well-designed and capable of handling the dynamic nature of SDN environments. With the right integration, configuration management can help maximize the flexibility, efficiency, and security of SDN-enabled networks, providing organizations with the tools they need to manage their infrastructure effectively and at scale.

The Future of Configuration Management Protocols

As the technological landscape continues to evolve, configuration management protocols are becoming increasingly vital in managing and maintaining the infrastructure of modern networks and systems. These protocols, which automate the process of configuring, deploying, and maintaining the consistency of devices and systems, have already proven their value in environments ranging from small-scale IT networks to large, complex enterprise infrastructures. However, as networks grow more dynamic, distributed, and complex, the future of configuration management will see significant changes, shaped by emerging trends in automation, cloud computing, security, and scalability.

The future of configuration management protocols will undoubtedly be driven by the need for greater automation and orchestration. As organizations face growing complexity in their IT environments, manual configuration management becomes increasingly untenable. The integration of artificial intelligence (AI) and machine learning (ML) into configuration management tools is already beginning to revolutionize how these systems function. These technologies can analyze vast amounts of data, identify patterns, and make predictive decisions about network configurations. For example, AI-powered configuration management systems could automatically adjust configurations based on real-time network conditions, security threats, or performance metrics. This would not only reduce the burden on network administrators but also enable organizations to respond to network demands faster and more efficiently. Machine learning algorithms could be used to detect configuration drift, predict potential failures, and recommend optimizations for network devices, further enhancing the automation of configuration management processes.

As organizations increasingly adopt cloud computing, the role of cloud-native configuration management protocols will expand. Cloud infrastructure, with its dynamic nature and on-demand resource provisioning, demands flexible and scalable configuration management systems that can handle the complexity of managing resources spread across multiple clouds, data centers, and hybrid environments. Future configuration management protocols will need to seamlessly integrate with cloud services and platforms, such as Amazon Web Services (AWS), Microsoft Azure, and Google Cloud, as well as containerized environments like Kubernetes. These protocols will allow administrators to manage configurations not just on physical devices but also on virtual machines, containers, and serverless computing resources, all while maintaining consistency, security, and compliance. Tools such as Terraform and Kubernetes already exemplify this shift, enabling infrastructure as code (IaC) and automating the configuration of cloud-based resources. As this trend continues, the future of configuration management will likely focus more on multi-cloud and hybrid-cloud environments, where protocols will need to support configuration management across diverse platforms and vendors.

The shift towards a more decentralized and distributed network architecture will also shape the future of configuration management protocols. The rise of edge computing and the Internet of Things (IoT) has led to a proliferation of connected devices that span everything from sensors and wearables to smart homes and autonomous vehicles. These devices are often deployed in remote or hard-to-reach locations, making it difficult to apply traditional configuration management methods. In the future, configuration management protocols will need to evolve to manage this highly distributed landscape. They will require enhanced capabilities for managing configurations on a massive scale, where devices may have intermittent connectivity or operate in environments with limited bandwidth and processing power. To meet these challenges, configuration management systems will likely integrate with lightweight protocols that are designed for low-resource devices, ensuring that configurations are automatically deployed and maintained even in challenging environments.

Security will continue to be a critical aspect of configuration management in the future. As organizations face an increasing number of cyber threats and regulatory requirements, ensuring the security of network configurations will be paramount. Misconfigurations remain one of the leading causes of security vulnerabilities, and as more devices become interconnected, the risk of attack increases. The future of configuration management will focus heavily on embedding security best practices directly into the configuration process. This will involve enforcing security policies automatically, ensuring that devices are configured with secure settings from the outset, and applying regular security updates and patches without delay. Moreover, security features such as encryption, identity and access management, and authentication mechanisms will become integral parts of configuration management protocols. Configuration management tools will be designed to automatically enforce compliance with security standards such as GDPR, HIPAA, and PCI-DSS, while also continuously monitoring configurations for any deviations that could indicate potential security risks.

Another significant development in the future of configuration management is the further integration of version control and change management practices. As networks become more dynamic, keeping track of changes to configurations becomes increasingly complex. Future configuration management protocols will place a greater emphasis on the ability to audit and track every change made to the network configuration. This will involve enhanced integration with version control systems such as Git, which will allow for the management of configuration files in a way that is similar to software development practices. The ability to roll back to previous configurations, track the history of changes, and collaborate on configuration files will become essential features of configuration management protocols. This versioning system will help organizations maintain a clear record of changes, ensuring that any misconfigurations can be quickly identified and corrected, reducing the potential impact of network disruptions.

With the growth of containerization and microservices architectures, configuration management protocols will need to adapt to these new paradigms. Containers, which are lightweight and portable, allow for rapid scaling and flexible deployment, but they also introduce new challenges in managing configurations. The dynamic nature of containerized environments, where containers are frequently created and destroyed, requires configuration management tools that can handle these frequent changes and maintain consistency across the environment. In the future, configuration management protocols will likely evolve to fully support containerized environments, enabling administrators to manage configurations for containers, microservices, and serverless functions with the same level of control and automation as traditional network devices.

Another trend shaping the future of configuration management is the increasing focus on self-healing networks. As networks grow in size and complexity, the likelihood of failures or misconfigurations increases. To address this, the future of configuration management will involve the development of self-healing capabilities that automatically detect and correct configuration issues. Using real-time monitoring, AI, and machine learning, networks will be able to identify misconfigurations or performance issues and automatically apply corrective configurations without human intervention. This approach will significantly reduce downtime, improve network reliability, and enhance the overall user experience by ensuring that network issues are addressed immediately as they arise.

The future of configuration management protocols is marked by a continued emphasis on automation, scalability, security, and adaptability. As networks become more complex, distributed, and dynamic, configuration management systems must evolve to manage not only traditional devices but also virtual, containerized, and IoT-enabled environments. Automation will play a central role in ensuring that configurations are deployed efficiently and consistently, while enhanced security features will help mitigate the risks posed by misconfigurations. Moreover, the integration of machine learning and AI will enable configuration management protocols to predict network needs, automatically adjust configurations, and proactively address issues before they impact performance or security. As the digital landscape continues to evolve, configuration management will remain a cornerstone of network operations, enabling organizations to maintain control, security, and efficiency in an increasingly complex world.

Case Studies in Configuration Management Protocol Implementation

Configuration management protocols play a critical role in ensuring the consistency, security, and efficiency of network configurations across diverse IT infrastructures. With the increasing complexity of modern networks, organizations are turning to these protocols to automate and streamline the management of network devices and services. The implementation of configuration management protocols can vary widely depending on the size of the organization, the type of network, and the specific goals of the deployment. By examining case studies of real-world implementations, it is possible to understand the practical challenges, benefits, and outcomes of using configuration management protocols in different environments.

One compelling case study comes from a large financial institution that faced significant challenges in managing its growing IT infrastructure. The company was operating with a highly distributed network of servers, routers, switches, and firewalls spread across multiple data centers. Over time, maintaining consistency in configuration across all these devices became increasingly difficult. Misconfigurations were common, leading to network outages, security vulnerabilities, and prolonged downtime during critical periods. The organization decided to implement an automated configuration management solution using Puppet to address these challenges. Puppet allowed the IT team to define standardized configuration templates for all network devices, ensuring that configurations were applied consistently across the network. By automating the configuration process, the company was able to reduce human error, increase efficiency, and significantly cut down on the time spent managing device configurations. The use of version control and real-time monitoring also helped the team detect configuration drift, ensuring that devices remained aligned with the organization's security policies and operational standards. The implementation of Puppet resulted in improved uptime, a more secure network, and a more streamlined process for managing and auditing configurations.

A different case study comes from a telecommunications company that needed to manage a vast and complex network of devices across multiple geographic regions. This company relied on a combination of traditional hardware and newer, cloud-based infrastructure, and its network was experiencing frequent performance issues due to inconsistent configurations across various devices. The company decided to implement Ansible, an open-source automation tool, to manage its network configurations. Ansible's agentless design made it an ideal choice for the company's hybrid environment, where devices ran on various operating systems and platforms. The company used Ansible to automate the deployment of configurations across its network, ensuring that security policies, software versions, and network settings were consistently applied. With Ansible's playbooks, the company was able to define configuration templates for different device types, which could be applied across the network with a single command. This not only improved consistency but also reduced the time needed to apply updates and patches to network devices. As a result, the company saw a reduction in network outages, faster deployment times for new services, and improved network performance.

In a smaller, more agile environment, a case study involving a cloud service provider highlights how configuration management protocols can be used to manage the complexities of cloud-based networks. The company operated a fully virtualized network infrastructure, with a mix of virtual machines, containers, and cloud services. One of the primary challenges was ensuring that configurations were kept in sync across the different platforms and that new resources were provisioned automatically in accordance with the company's best practices. The company implemented Terraform, an open-source infrastructure-as-code (IaC) tool, in conjunction with its cloud services to automate the deployment of resources and network configurations. Terraform allowed the company to define its network infrastructure as code, which was then stored in version-controlled repositories and automatically deployed to the cloud environment. With this setup, the company was able to reduce the time spent manually configuring new virtual machines and containers, ensuring that resources were deployed quickly and consistently. Furthermore, Terraform's integration with the cloud service provider's APIs allowed for automatic scaling and configuration updates, which were applied without manual intervention. This implementation resulted in a more flexible, scalable, and efficient cloud environment, with fewer configuration errors and faster service delivery to customers.

In another example, a manufacturing company that had deployed a large IoT network faced challenges related to the management of its numerous IoT devices. These devices were distributed across factory floors, warehouses, and remote locations, and the company needed a way to ensure that all devices were securely configured and maintained. The organization chose to implement Chef, a popular configuration management tool, to automate the configuration and management of its IoT devices. Chef's ability to handle complex configurations and integrate with various IoT platforms made it a natural choice for this environment. The company used Chef to define device configurations, such as security settings, network access controls, and firmware versions, and then deployed these configurations to devices remotely. This allowed the company to ensure that all IoT devices were compliant with security policies and maintained the same operational standards. By automating the configuration process, the company was able to scale its IoT network quickly while maintaining security and consistency across the devices. Additionally, Chef's ability to integrate with monitoring systems provided real-time visibility into the status of devices, allowing administrators to quickly detect and resolve any issues that arose.

Another case study from a large healthcare organization demonstrates how configuration management protocols can help ensure compliance with industry regulations. In the healthcare industry, maintaining the privacy and security of patient data is a top priority, and regulatory frameworks such as HIPAA mandate strict requirements for data protection. The organization was managing a large number of servers, databases, and medical devices that were subject to these regulations. The challenge was to ensure that configurations were regularly updated to meet compliance standards, while also minimizing downtime and disruptions to patient services. The organization implemented SaltStack, a powerful configuration management and automation tool, to automate the deployment of security patches and configuration updates across its network. SaltStack allowed the IT team to define compliance templates that included security policies, encryption standards, and user access controls, which were automatically applied to devices and systems across the organization. The use of SaltStack's audit and reporting features also provided the organization with an easy way to track and demonstrate compliance during audits. This implementation not only improved compliance with regulatory requirements but also reduced the time and resources needed to manually manage configurations, ultimately leading to a more secure and efficient IT environment.

In each of these case studies, the implementation of configuration management protocols brought about significant improvements in the management, security, and efficiency of the networks and systems. Whether dealing with a large enterprise network, a hybrid cloud environment, or a distributed IoT network, the benefits of automation, consistency, and real-time monitoring were evident. Configuration management protocols allowed these organizations to standardize their configurations, reduce errors, and ensure that network devices and services were always up-to-date and secure. The common theme across these case studies is that the successful integration of configuration management tools not only simplifies network operations but also enhances the organization's ability to scale, improve performance, and maintain compliance with industry standards. As networks continue to grow in complexity and scale, the importance of effective configuration management protocols will only increase, offering organizations a powerful way to keep their IT environments secure, reliable, and efficient.

Conclusion: Enhancing Network Efficiency through Configuration Management Protocols

In the world of modern network administration, ensuring the smooth operation of networks, systems, and devices is paramount. As organizations scale their networks and move toward more dynamic, decentralized environments, the need for efficient, secure, and consistent configuration management has never been more critical. Configuration management protocols have evolved to address these needs, offering powerful tools that automate and streamline the process of configuring, deploying, and maintaining network devices and systems. These protocols not only simplify administrative tasks but also enhance network performance, security, and reliability, allowing businesses to focus on growth and innovation without being bogged down by the complexities of managing increasingly sophisticated infrastructures.

At the core of configuration management is the ability to automate the management of network devices and services, ensuring that configurations are consistently applied across diverse environments. As networks become more complex, manual configuration management processes are increasingly impractical and error-prone. The integration of configuration management protocols, such as Ansible, Puppet, Chef, and SaltStack, into modern network environments has allowed administrators to define configurations once and deploy them automatically across multiple devices, locations, and even clouds. Automation reduces human error and increases efficiency, enabling administrators to apply security patches, updates, and configuration changes at scale, in a fraction of the time it would take through manual processes. These protocols facilitate the rapid deployment of network devices and services, allowing organizations to adapt quickly to changing business needs and market demands.

In large-scale networks, the benefits of using configuration management protocols are especially apparent. As organizations grow and their IT infrastructures expand, ensuring consistency and compliance across all devices becomes a monumental task. Configuration management protocols enable administrators to establish standard configurations for all devices and systems, ensuring that every network component adheres to the same operational and security policies. This consistency reduces the risk of misconfigurations, which are a leading cause of network outages and security vulnerabilities. Furthermore, automated configuration deployment makes it possible to keep all devices up-to-date with the latest security patches, software updates, and configuration settings, ensuring that the network remains secure and operational at all times.

The importance of security in modern networks cannot be overstated. As cyber threats become more sophisticated, organizations must adopt proactive measures to safeguard their networks from vulnerabilities. Misconfigurations are one of the most common causes of security breaches, and ensuring that every network device is configured securely is a critical part of any network security strategy. Configuration management protocols allow administrators to enforce security policies automatically, applying strong encryption, access controls, and other security settings consistently across the network. By embedding security best practices into the configuration process, organizations can reduce the risk of vulnerabilities caused by human error or outdated configurations. Real-time monitoring and auditing features in many configuration management tools also enable administrators to detect and correct security issues as soon as they arise, further enhancing the network's resilience to attacks.

Another significant advantage of configuration management protocols is their ability to improve network performance. Network performance can be heavily influenced by the configuration of individual devices, such as routers, switches, firewalls, and load balancers. A misconfigured device can cause network bottlenecks, degraded performance, or even complete service disruptions. Configuration management protocols ensure that devices are consistently configured to meet the performance requirements of the organization. By automating the configuration of network devices based on predefined templates, administrators can ensure that devices are set up to optimize network traffic flow, minimize latency, and handle increasing demands as the network scales. Additionally, automated configuration management allows for real-time adjustments, enabling administrators to quickly respond to performance issues or changes in network traffic patterns.

The scalability of configuration management protocols is another key factor in enhancing network efficiency. As networks grow, so too does the complexity of managing configurations across a larger number of devices, services, and applications. Configuration management tools designed for scalability allow organizations to manage their growing infrastructures without compromising performance or reliability. By automating configuration deployment and updates, these tools enable organizations to scale their networks quickly and efficiently, ensuring that all devices are properly configured and remain aligned with organizational standards. Whether managing on-premises servers, cloud-based resources, or a combination of both, configuration management protocols provide the scalability needed to keep pace with the increasing demands of modern networks.

Moreover, configuration management protocols contribute to the overall agility of the organization. In today's fast-paced business environment, the ability to quickly adapt to new technologies, business models, or market conditions is essential. Configuration management protocols enable organizations to provision new network devices and services with ease, applying configurations in real-time to support rapid deployment. The automation of configuration tasks allows administrators to focus on more strategic initiatives, such as optimizing network performance or implementing new services, rather than spending time on routine maintenance and configuration updates. The flexibility and speed of configuration management tools allow organizations to move quickly, reduce downtime, and accelerate innovation.

One of the key trends in the future of configuration management is the integration of these protocols with cloud-native and containerized environments. As organizations increasingly adopt cloud technologies, including private, public, and hybrid cloud models, the need for configuration management tools that can handle the complexities of cloud-based networks becomes more pressing. The dynamic nature of cloud environments, where resources are provisioned and decommissioned at a rapid pace, requires configuration management protocols that can automatically adjust to changing network conditions. The rise of containerization and microservices further complicates the management of network configurations, as containers and services are frequently spun up and torn down. Modern configuration management tools are adapting to these challenges by offering solutions that integrate seamlessly with cloud platforms and container orchestration tools like Kubernetes. This integration enables organizations to automate configuration management for cloud-based resources, ensuring that networks remain consistent, secure, and efficient across both physical and virtual environments.

In addition to cloud and container management, the growing adoption of edge computing presents new opportunities and challenges for configuration management protocols. Edge computing extends computing resources to the edge of the network, closer to where data is generated, enabling real-time processing and reducing latency. As more devices and systems are deployed at the edge of the network, configuration management protocols must evolve to manage these distributed systems efficiently. Edge devices may have limited processing power and connectivity, which requires lightweight, flexible configuration management solutions that can operate effectively in these resource-constrained environments. The ability to manage configurations at scale across distributed, edge-based devices will be a key factor in the success of edge computing deployments.

The role of configuration management in enhancing network efficiency will only continue to grow as organizations adopt more advanced technologies and scale their infrastructures. Automation, security, scalability, and real-time monitoring will remain central to configuration management protocols, enabling organizations to manage their networks more effectively and efficiently. By reducing the risk of misconfigurations, improving security posture, optimizing performance, and enabling rapid deployment of network resources, configuration management tools provide the foundation for a more agile, secure, and reliable network. As the complexity of modern networks continues to increase, configuration management protocols will be essential in ensuring that networks operate smoothly, securely, and with minimal downtime, ultimately driving business success and technological advancement.

www.ingramcontent.com/pod-product-compliance
Lightning Source LLC
LaVergne TN
LVHW051231050326
832903LV00028B/2352